MINNEAPOLIS

MINNEAPOLIS

An Urban Biography

UPDATED EDITION

TOM WEBER

Minnesota Historical Society Press

MINNESOTA
HISTORICAL
SOCIETY PRESS

CLEAN
WATER
LAND &
LEGACY
AMENDMENT

Cities, like people, are always changing, and the history of that change
is the city's biography. The Urban Biography Series illuminates the unique character
of each city, weaving in the hidden stories of place, politics, and identity that
continue to shape its residents' lives.

mnhspress.org

The Minnesota Historical Society Press is a member of the Association of University Presses.

Manufactured in the United States of America

10 9 8 7 6 5 4 3 2 1

♾ The paper used in this publication meets the minimum requirements of
the American National Standard for Information Sciences—Permanence
for Printed Library Materials, ANSI Z39.48–1984.

International Standard Book Number
ISBN: 978-1-68134-260-3 (paper)
ISBN: 978-1-68134-263-4 (e-book)

Library of Congress Cataloging-in-Publication Data

Names: Weber, Tom (Thomas W.), author.
Title: Minneapolis : an urban biography / Tom Weber.
Description: Saint Paul : Minnesota Historical Society Press, [2020] |
Includes bibliographical references and index. | Summary: "A biography of Minneapolis,
the City of Lakes, starting with Bdote, the confluence of the Mississippi and the Minnesota
Rivers and a sacred place for Dakota people, who have lived here for millennia. Since the
city's beginnings in the 1850s, Minneapolis has experienced continual collapses and
rebuilding. Some collapses were real, as when the falls were nearly destroyed; some are
metaphorical, as when corruption and the mob threatened to overtake the life of the city.
The narrative highlights stories of immigrants, milling, the American Indian Movement,
the KKK, the university, business innovators, the vibrant arts and music scene,
powerful sports teams, and a wealth of other topics." —Provided by publisher.
Identifiers: LCCN 2020010195 | ISBN 9781681341613 (paperback) |
ISBN 9781681341620 (ebook)
Subjects: LCSH: Minneapolis (Minn.)—History.
Classification: LCC F614.M54 W43 2020 | DDC 977.6/579—dc23
LC record available at https://lccn.loc.gov/2020010195

This and other Minnesota Historical Society Press books are
available from popular e-book vendors.

To Peggy and Siobhan,
the kwe power that lights my life

Contents

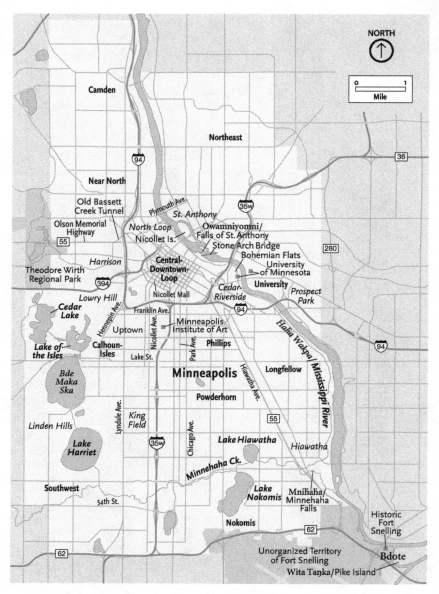

NORTH

Mile

Camden

Northeast

Near North

Old Bassett
Creek Tunnel

Olson Memorial
Highway

Plymouth Ave.

St. Anthony

North Loop
Nicollet Is.

Owamniyomni/
Falls of St. Anthony

Stone Arch Bridge

Bohemian Flats

University
of Minnesota

Harrison

Theodore Wirth
Regional Park

Central-
Downtown-
Loop

Nicollet Mall

University

Cedar-
Riverside

Prospect
Park

Lowry Hill

Cedar
Lake

Hennepin Ave.

Franklin Ave.

Minneapolis
Institute of Art

Lake of
the Isles

Uptown

Nicollet Ave.

Calhoun-
Isles

Lake St.

Phillips

Bde
Maka
Ska

Park Ave.

Minneapolis

Longfellow

Ȟaȟa Wakpa/Mississippi River

Linden Hills

King
Field

Lyndale Ave.

Powderhorn

Chicago Ave.

Hiawatha Ave.

Lake Harriet

Lake Hiawatha

Hiawatha

Southwest

54th St.

Minnehaha Ck.

Lake
Nokomis

Mnihaha/
Minnehaha
Falls

Historic
Fort
Snelling

Nokomis

Unorganized Territory
of Fort Snelling

Bdote

Wita Taŋka/Pike Island

Minneapolis is officially divided into eleven communities (labeled in boldface),
each containing several of the city's eighty-one neighborhoods (labeled in
italic). This map shows neighborhoods that are mentioned in the text. *Map by
Matt Kania, Map Hero Inc.*

Prologue

The euphoria was still there on Friday, October 30, 1987.

Five days earlier, the Minnesota Twins had won baseball's World Series. A massive parade—the biggest since a ticker-tape parade for President Harry Truman in 1948—drew two hundred thousand in Minneapolis, then another two hundred thousand when it moved to St. Paul. Many fans and players waved their Homer Hankies, which had debuted during the playoffs and were already becoming iconic memorabilia.

After the dynastic Minneapolis Lakers basketball team defected to Los Angeles in 1960, the arrival in 1961 of both baseball's Twins and football's Vikings kept valid—and even boosted—the region's claim as a big-league market for professional sports. Hockey's North Stars arrived in 1967. Unlike the Lakers of yore, none of these teams had won a championship. Until now.

But on that Friday morning, a very small group of people in the state were turning their focus away from the Twins. They were thinking about a vigil that would happen that evening and a ceremony the next morning, 125 years in the making.

In the winter of 1862–63, about sixteen hundred Dakota women, children, and elders were held at a concentration camp near Fort Snelling to await expulsion after the six-week US–Dakota War. Hundreds of them died there, mostly from measles and other diseases. The camp stood steps from the confluence of the Mississippi and Minnesota Rivers, which is a sacred place of creation for many of the Dakota, who call it Bdote. These Dakota were imprisoned within sight of what they considered the center of Earth and of all things, their most revered spot on the planet.

One of Chris Cavender's ancestors, Haza Wiŋ (Blueberry Woman), had been a prisoner. He spoke at the events, held on the same floodplain where the camp once stood: a wooded area next to a parking lot in what was now a state park. As elders spoke, the fort loomed atop the nearby ridge and planes passed overhead, heading to and from the nearby international airport. The names of those held at the camp were read aloud; drummers closed with honor songs.

The event wasn't universally heralded among Dakota people. "Unless there are reparations, what's the point?" asked one descendent of the leader Little Crow who didn't attend. But for those who did, it was important the state was acknowledging that this had happened—tangible evidence, Cavender said at the time, "that the Dakota were people, that they were human beings with feelings and dignity."

During the same week in October 1987, two locations fewer than ten miles apart had hosted one of the area's brightest and most unifying events, while also marking one of its darkest chapters.

Governor Rudy Perpich had declared 1987 a Year of Reconciliation in remembering the US–Dakota War. Cavender, who has since taken the Dakota name Chris Mato Nunpa, reflected years later that no real reconciliation happened: "Justice also has to happen before we can talk about reconciliation. And that means economic justice, including payments for treaties that still haven't been paid." St. Paul mayor George Latimer was probably more accurate when he said 1987 would be remembered as "the year the Twins stole the heart of every Minnesotan."

This is the whiplash of Minneapolis's story.

Each month brings a bevy of accolades, lauding Minneapolis as one of the nation's greenest, healthiest, most literate, LGBTQIA+-friendly, bike-friendly, dog-friendly cities. We have the best parks, and the best music, food, and beer scenes. It's one of the best places to live—a well-kept secret, really. And have you seen our awesome airport?

The same month also brings the latest evidence of how unaffordable the city's housing is; how unwelcoming it can be to newcomers; and how crippling the disparities are when you measure these things by race. Minneapolis is home to some of the largest—sometimes *the* largest—gaps between how healthy or academically successful white people are compared to Black, brown, and Indigenous peoples. A lower percentage of African Americans own homes in the Twin Cities than in any metro area in the country.

This whiplash was baked into Minneapolis since before its founding in 1867. No state seemed more behind preserving the Union and ending slavery in 1860, when Minnesotans cast the second-highest percentage of votes for Abraham Lincoln than voters in any other state. It was the first state to volunteer soldiers to the Union effort when the Civil War started. Then, a year later, Minnesota's concentration camp was built, followed by the expulsion of all Dakota and Ho-Chunk peoples. In 1909, with slavery abolished and Minneapolis on the right side of history, a race riot started by whites in Prospect Park signaled the beginning of a new generation of real estate contracts that kept people of color from buying homes.

Minneapolis exists where it does because of St. Anthony Falls. The Dakota call it Owamniyomni. The falls—now cloaked in a concrete apron, a whiplash of a different kind—fueled industries that separated the city from any other between Chicago and Seattle. The timber and flour industries provided markets and jobs for farmers, lumberjacks, and laborers throughout the Upper Midwest.

The Minneapolis whiplash exists here, where Pillsburys and Washburns made their fortunes and built corporate industrial giants that created offshoot markets for prosthetic limb businesses because so many people lost body parts on the job. A mile downriver, the immigrants who lived in the flood-prone Bohemian Flats fed themselves, in part, by snagging floating fruit discarded upstream. Even the river is part of the whiplash: it was a crucial part of the city's growth and success, until it wasn't. So we turned our backs on the river, until we didn't.

A significant part of Minneapolis's story happened even before 1867, some of it outside modern city limits. While Fort Snelling isn't technically part of the city, the imposing stone structure established the US presence in the area, essential to future colonization. The soldiers' use of waterpower at the falls demonstrated its tantalizing value for later exploitation. And the story of the US–Dakota War is crucial to understanding how Minneapolitans participated in the taking of the land base that permitted the city's growth.

Minneapolis has a history of collapses and rebuilding. Some collapses were real, as when the falls were nearly destroyed; others were metaphoric, as when corruption and the mob threatened to overtake the city's workings until a progressive movement gained steam and, later, a young mayor named Humphrey did something different.

And yet, even as we always have rebuilt, it's worth asking who was in charge of rebuilding—who was left in and left out, and how did those decisions leave us with the whiplash we have today.

This urban biography is a story of some people doing big and important things and of others doing relatively small things that had big implications. The following chapters approach the city's history through place and theme, rather than through strict chronology. Some overlap, others are complementary, and all add to an understanding of the complex history of Minneapolis. The overarching goal is to take what may be the most significant issue facing contemporary Minneapolis—the crippling disparities among its people, exposed to the world in 2020, after the murder of George Floyd—and present a history that examines why those disparities exist, even as the city makes a legitimate argument for itself as a must-visit or must-live kind of place.

For Minneapolitans seeking solutions to these inequities and disparities, to ignore the city's history of discrimination, racism, and inequality is to condemn such an effort to failure.

CHAPTER 1

Bdote

The difference between Indigenous people and settlers is that
Indigenous people have origin stories and creation stories, and settlers
have colonization stories. That is the stark difference . . . that
relationship to land and being of the land, coming *from* the land versus
coming *to* it in a process of settling.

—Dr. Adrienne Keene, *All My Relations* podcast, February 26, 2019

Long before the water was sacred to the Native Americans who lived here, and long before settler-colonists gave their town a name that translates to "water city," the water was everywhere, and it was frozen.

During Earth's most recent ice age, glaciers covered most of Minnesota. About twelve thousand years ago, when that ice age ended, the melting and floods that followed carved the land in ways that would determine the exact location of the future Minneapolis. Woolly mammoths may have gathered near the river on the lovely plain that would later become a gathering spot for Homo sapiens on a Saturday night.

In between the time of the glaciers and construction of Hennepin Avenue, Native Americans lived here for millennia, utilizing the rivers that made this a key place for trade and transportation. A grave in this area that dates to at least six thousand years ago included an artifact made from a conch shell from present-day Florida. Indigenous nations that cite Minnesota in their histories at one time or another include the Cheyenne, the Oceti Ṡakowiŋ (historically known to Europeans as the Sioux, including the Dakota people), the Ho-Chunk (Winnebago), the Báxoǰe (Iowa), the Ojibwe (Chippewa, Anishinaabe), and the Oto. By the 1600s, the Dakota and Ojibwe were the main peoples living across present-day Minnesota.

The Ojibwe originated in northeastern North America, including present-day Quebec, and migrated west over hundreds of years. Minnesota's seven Ojibwe tribal reservations today are all located north of Interstate 94 (I-94), but their pre-European settlement history also places them in what would become the Twin Cities area. The Anishinaabe and Dakota have at times been at war, but they have lived more often in peace throughout their history, including as partners during the fur trade era.

The Dakota have the deepest connection to the present-day Twin Cities region. They are the only Indigenous people who have lived in this area who have never claimed any other land as their ancestral home, and they claim the ancient inhabitants of the land as their ancestors. Other peoples migrated here from elsewhere. The Dakota were on this land for thousands of years before the arrival of settler-colonists—people who intended to take their land and replace them—and the Dakota language remains in many place-names, including Minnesota and Minneapolis. The state is named for the river Mni Sota—translated as "waters so clear they reflect the clouds." Minneapolis combines the Dakota word for water, "mni," with the Greek word for city, "polis." Mni-polis.

The Dakota belong to the Oceti Śakowiŋ, the Seven Council Fires. Linguistically called Siouan or "Sioux" by outsiders, the bands are divided among Dakota, Nakota, and Lakota. Four of the seven council fires make up the Eastern Dakota, and they originate in Minnesota and the surrounding region. The Dakota and remaining middle and western bands (the Nakota and Lakota) also stretch across the Dakotas, Nebraska, Montana, and into Canada. The Oceti Śakowiŋ have many creation stories. The most significant and widely held in this region is that the Dakota were brought by the Creator from the stars to the place where the Mni Sota Wakpa (Minnesota) and Haha Wakpa (Mississippi) Rivers meet. That confluence today includes Fort Snelling, which is often called the birthplace of Minnesota. But for uncounted generations, this confluence also has been known as Bdote.

Bdote translates to "where two waters come together," and confluences are common in this well-watered land. But this confluence—Bdote Mni Sota—has a deeper, spiritual meaning for many Dakota people. It's a sacred place that is nothing less than the beginning of everything. Missionary Stephen R. Riggs, who began trying to convert the Dakota in 1837, wrote, "The Mdewakanton [the easternmost of the Seven Council Fires] think that the mouth of the Minnesota River is precisely over the center of the earth, and that they occupy the gate that opens into the western world."

The confluence occurs at what is now called Pike Island. The Dakota name for the island is Wita Taŋka, and many Dakota believe it was at this spot where the Creator first made people. Today, the island is officially part of St. Paul and Fort Snelling State Park, where visitors can hike, ski, and go birding throughout the year—when there's no flooding.

Fort Snelling, an 1850 oil painting by Henry Lewis showing Wita Taŋka and Bdote with Fort Snelling in the background. *MNHS Collections*

Opposite the confluence is Oheyawahe (Pilot Knob), renamed Wota-kuye Paha (Hill of All the Relatives) in 2004. It was and is a place of burial and medicine ceremony for the Dakota, and it was also a place where Dakota, Ojibwe, and Báxoje peoples gathered. Later, the land oppo-site Bdote became an important settlement among settler-colonists. It housed, among other things, the headquarters for the American Fur Company, which at one time controlled the fur trade throughout Minnesota. The area also was initially proposed as the location for the capital of the Minnesota territory, though that was soon changed to St. Paul.

Extended families and kinship have always been a pillar on which Dakota culture rested. As Dakota anthropologist Ella Deloria notes, "The ultimate aim of Dakota life . . . was quite simple: One must obey kin-ship rules; one must be a good relative." Extended families, where the brother of a father was thought of as a father, helped provide health and safety for a family and the community. This practice of the inclusive, extended family was called tioṡpaye. The word "mitakuyapi," used in traditional Dakota greetings, translates to "all my relatives." Hau, mita-kuyapi. Hello, my relatives.

Even the land is considered a mother—an actual relative. This helps explain the pain and trauma caused later, when European Americans took the land: for the settler-colonists, it was a real estate transaction; for the Dakota, it was the loss of a relative.

Dakota families moved throughout the year, but calling them nomadic suggests aimless wandering. Rather, they moved in purposeful cycles with the seasons, keeping an important connection to the land and its riches. In the summer villages, Dakota women grew corn and gathered berries and other foods. When men left on hunting and fishing parties, women, who were considered strong leaders and partners in society, managed life in the home community and cared for elders and chil-dren. This role was held in high esteem. Families moved to places for harvesting wild rice in the late summer; places for deer hunting in the fall; and places where smaller family groups stayed in the winter before moving in the spring to places for harvesting maple sugar.

Sacred places throughout the area of Bdote were used for ceremonies. A natural spring not far from Bdote, Mni Sni (Coldwater Spring), was the home of the water spirit; Dakota people met visiting Ojibwe and other Native peoples there. Burial mounds crowned the bluffs above the river. A short way up Ḣaḣa Wakpa (the Mississippi River), the magnificent waterfall known as Owamniyomni (meaning "whirlpool") was a sacred place, as were Wanaġi Wita (Spirit Island) and other islands near it. Nearby Wita Waṡte (Nicollet Island) was a place for sugaring and also where women went to give birth. Owamniyomni would be renamed St. Anthony Falls and come to define Minneapolis as a lumber and milling giant; Spirit Island was later quarried into near oblivion for its limestone before being removed in 1960 to make way for a lock.

Of course, the frame of Minneapolis geography does not work well for telling Dakota history. The city's boundaries, made final in 1927, encompass a small part of the Dakota homeland. Bdote, so central to any story of the people who lived here before there was a Minneapolis, is not in fact part of the city. Fort Snelling and the nearby international

St. Anthony Falls, 1786 shows Owamniyomni as Alexis Jean Fournier imagined and painted it in oil a century later, in 1887. *MNHS Collections*

airport are in an "Unorganized Territory"—part of Hennepin County, but not part of any city. Although many people may see the area as part of Minneapolis, a host of local, state, and federal governments exact various measures of control over the land and water. State and regional parks line the waters at the confluence. While no tribal nations have any direct control over the area today, they continue to participate in public conversations, trying to be a voice for the land.

They Arrive

The same waterways that were places of ceremony and means of transportation for Indigenous peoples brought Europeans to the region. French and British traders and missionaries would use these routes, including the Great Lakes to the north, as would US soldiers and others with trade and occupation in mind.

Father Louis Hennepin, a Franciscan priest from what is now Belgium, had been sent to North America to explore French colonies. After first seeing Niagara Falls in 1678—which he described in writings as "this horrible Precipice"—Hennepin then headed west to look for ways to expand the fur trade into what was then part of New France and to seek the source of the Mississippi River.

Hennepin and two other Frenchmen had traveled as captives of the Dakota (or perhaps as guests; perspectives differed) to Mille Lacs, then down the Rum River to the Mississippi. On this return trip, in July 1680, Hennepin first saw the falls, which he named for St. Anthony of Padua in what river historian John Anfinson describes as the "first act of occupation in what would become the Twin Cities."

From there, the history of European arrival includes eventual claims to the land by France, Britain, and Spain, though Spain focused on colonizing to the south. France and Britain did not want to establish large-scale settlements; they wanted to build small posts throughout the region to get into the business of fur. Fur-bearing animals had been hunted nearly to extinction in Europe, and their pelts were valuable. Indigenous families trapped and processed the pelts of beaver, muskrats, and many other small animals; European traders exchanged blankets, metal tools, brass kettles, firearms, and ammunition for them.

The French, who arrived first, knew they needed friendly relationships with Native Americans to survive. A marriage to an Indigenous woman meant her relatives would be your relatives, and would support and trade with you. This gave the Ojibwe and Dakota some power. Gradually, intermarriage increased between the European Americans and Natives. Children of these unions often bridged relationships between European Americans and Indigenous peoples.

In 1754, the French and Indian War began between France and Britain. The Treaty of Paris ended that war in 1763 and further shuffled colonial holdings. At one point, the land that would become the future Twin Cities (and the future Minnesota) was split between the two European powers. British military officers and traders arrived to take over the land claims; the Indigenous peoples met them with varying degrees of skepticism and hostility, as they had the French. One key difference, though, is that the British had distinct practices around credit and who could open a trade business. This ended up increasing debts among Native peoples. Debt repayment became a significant motivation for future treaties in which Indigenous peoples signed over rights to their land.

In 1783, when the American colonies defeated the British, the new United States included all former British claims that weren't already colonies. Everything in future Minnesota east of the Mississippi became the northwestern-most part of the Northwest Territory. In 1804, the United States paid the French $15 million for the Louisiana Purchase, which brought most of the rest of future Minnesota (west of the Mississippi) under the claim of the United States. Of course, Indigenous peoples had no say in these deals, which initially meant little to them in their day-to-day lives.

Louisiana was a vast addition to the United States—part or all of fifteen future states and two future Canadian provinces. Expeditions to map and explore the purchase area soon followed. Meriwether Lewis and William Clark went west. Zebulon Pike went north.

Pike

Pike was an inexperienced, twenty-six-year-old army lieutenant. He was sent up the Mississippi River from St. Louis with orders to find the headwaters of the Mississippi and also good locations for military installations, specifically at the Mississippi's confluence with the St. Peter's River, as the Minnesota River was then known, and at St. Anthony Falls. He was also told to establish friendly relations with the Dakota and Ojibwe and research British trading in the area, which had continued unabated since the end of the American Revolution. British flags, in fact, were still flying over some posts.

After being received warmly by Dakota leaders along the way, Pike arrived at Wita Taŋka, the island that would one day bear his name, and made camp on September 21, 1805. Just two days later, seven Dakota leaders and their men met with Pike on the island. There, Pike prepared a document that granted the United States land for military posts at Bdote and up the Mississippi to St. Anthony Falls; its provisions included a promise to build a government factory, or trading post. The agreement also promised payment to the Dakota for the land, though the amount was left blank. The final section affirmed that the Dakota had the right to travel and use the land as they had before.

This document, which became known as Pike's Treaty, is a perfect illustration of how differently Indigenous peoples would have interpreted documents they signed with the United States. From the Dakota perspective, there might have seemed little to lose from an agreement that still let them use the land as they always had. Also, building a new post meant more trading. As such, it is unlikely that Dakota leaders and Pike's party had the same understanding of the transaction. For Dakota people, land wasn't ownable. It was a relative.

Then, as quickly as he had come to Wita Taŋka, Pike left and headed north. He made it to Leech Lake, which he mistakenly identified as the headwaters of the Mississippi (though he was only about twenty-five miles off). He came back through the next year en route to St. Louis, encountering an April snowstorm at St. Anthony Falls and trying at Bdote to encourage Dakota leaders to accompany him south—to no avail.

The Pike expedition found nothing that hadn't already been seen, reported, or named, even by Europeans and Americans. His days at Bdote might very well have been forgotten by many Dakota as soon as he left. They went back to trading with the British, and it would be several years before there was any further substantial contact with the United States.

It would be easy to dismiss Pike's trip as a junior varsity version of what Lewis and Clark were doing at the same time. In addition to his lackluster achievements, Pike was, according to historian W. E. Hollon, doubtlessly "naive, egotistical, and extremely ambitious." Bdote was a stopover for Pike, albeit an important one, and the entire time he spent in the area totaled about two weeks. But the trip represented the Dakota people's first official contact with a US government representative. And Pike had set in motion the eventual creation of Fort Snelling and the Minneapolis–St. Paul region we know today.

US senators didn't consider Pike's treaty until 1808, three years after the meeting at Bdote. During deliberations, they added acreage and the amount of $2,000 to the treaty, even though Pike had valued the land in question at one hundred times that. However, no Dakota were in Washington during those debates and no Dakota agreed to those changes. In addition, President Thomas Jefferson did not proclaim the treaty after it was ratified, a standard step at the time that made a treaty official. Thus, some histories suggest the one hundred thousand acres that eventually became the core of Minneapolis was bought with nothing more than the $200 in goods, including liquor, that Pike personally gifted that day, along with $2,000 that would be distributed in 1819.

But there are other reasons to question the document's validity. Only two of the seven Dakota leaders present that day signed the treaty. Dakota people made important decisions by consensus, and the two did not represent all Dakota who had cultural claims to the area. There were also validity questions on the US side: because the president had not authorized Pike's expedition, the lieutenant had no authority to negotiate treaties. Pike had actually been sent by the US Army's senior general, James Wilkinson, who was also the new territorial governor of Louisiana. After his death, Wilkinson was found to have been a traitor, sharing US secrets as a spy for Spain.

Half a century later, the US Senate's Military Affairs Committee, still pondering the treaty, noted Pike had made the agreement with just two men and that "there is no evidence that this agreement, to which there is not even a witness, and in which no consideration was named, was ever considered binding upon the Indians, or that they ever yielded up the possession of their lands under it." That mattered little, however, when the army showed up fourteen years later to start what Pike had ostensibly negotiated to do: build a fort. As such, Fort Snelling, which would become known as the birthplace of Minnesota, was built using justification written into a flawed and likely invalid document.

Fort Snelling

In the late 1810s—after Pike's expedition and after the War of 1812—Minnesota was considered part of the western United States, but on paper only. The war had demonstrated the nation's vulnerability to the west: had the British seized control of the river, the United States would have been effectively encircled. There was no real US power being exercised; there weren't even that many Americans around. In addition, there was real money to be made by whoever controlled the region's fur trade. That's why Secretary of War John C. Calhoun oversaw an effort to build forts in the area, writing, "When these posts are all established and occupied . . . our northwestern frontier will be rendered much more secure than heretofore, and . . . the most valuable fur trade in the world will be thrown into our hands." Lieutenant Colonel Henry Leavenworth and nearly one hundred men arrived in 1819 to begin construction of what was then known as Fort St. Anthony. With the group was a US Indian agent who distributed $2,000 in goods to the Dakota as payment under the terms of the Pike treaty, even though the Dakota had never agreed to that amount. The fort was later renamed for Colonel

Josiah Snelling, who arrived in 1820 to supervise and get back on track what became a five-year construction project.

The US government's presence in the region was far from influential or imperial—and that first winter would prove brutal, demoralizing, and even fatal to some in the group—but the occupation had begun. The area around Bdote at this time was still a place where French was the language generally used by European and Indigenous traders. While the government's presence at the fort was initially economic, the fort was nevertheless a decidedly military structure intended to expel British fur traders from the area and to keep settler-colonists off Indigenous land until the US government could secure the land for colonization through treaties.

Minnesota Slavery

In 1820, the Missouri Compromise banned slavery north of the 36°30′ parallel, which included Minnesota. But it was well known that influential fur traders like Jean-Baptiste Faribault and army officers, including Colonel Snelling and others, owned enslaved African Americans. While the number of enslaved people in the area was small, an army voucher system actually *incentivized* slavery by giving officers extra pay to have servants, which was interpreted to include enslaved people.

The most famous US Supreme Court ruling on slavery, *Dred Scott v. Sandford*, started at Fort Snelling, when Harriet Robinson married Dred Scott in 1836. Robinson had been owned by US Indian Agent Lawrence Taliaferro, the largest slaveholder at the fort at the time. When Dred Scott's enslaver, Dr. John Emerson, moved to St. Louis, the couple moved with him.

The Scotts became the property of Emerson's wife after his death. And it was in St. Louis that Harriet Scott pushed her husband to sue, using the fact they had lived at Fort Snelling as their basis for why they should win their freedom.

Also under consideration were the Scotts' daughters, who would soon be ten, an age that fetched more on the market for enslaved people. Harriet Scott wanted to keep the family together. The Supreme Court ruled in 1857 that enslaved people were property; they could be moved between free and slave territories with no change in status. Justices also ruled enslaved African Americans couldn't sue in federal court because they weren't citizens.

The Dred Scott ruling also conflicted with previous cases in which two women enslaved at Fort Snelling—known only as Rachel and Courtney—had won their freedom in Missouri courts. The Rachel and Courtney cases affirmed that slavery was illegal in the territory. In theory, this should have stopped the practice.

Rachel and Courtney won their freedom just a month after Dred Scott had arrived at the fort. The Dred Scott ruling—which pushed the country closer to civil war and which also helped raise the political profile of a former one-term congressman from Illinois named Abraham Lincoln—might never have happened if the officers and fur traders at Bdote had taken the Rachel and Courtney rulings to heart.

In October 1857, seven months after the Dred Scott ruling and a year after violence over the slavery issue had broken out in Kansas—earning it the name "Bleeding Kansas"—voters in the Minnesota territory overwhelmingly approved a constitution, a necessary step toward becoming a state. The constitution included a ban on slavery. When Minnesota was admitted into the Union as a free state the following May, the legal landscape had changed. But it wasn't legalities that finally drove slavery out of Fort Snelling; it was the transfer of its last slaveholding army unit to Utah in 1857.

Fort Snelling closed in 1858, but the start of the Civil War two years later gave it new life. Nearly twenty-five thousand soldiers trained there from 1861 to 1865. But for the Civil War, the fort's history would have ended.

The War and the Concentration Camp

The sordid chapter of Minnesota's concentration camp was years in the making, and it continues to resonate among Minneapolis residents today. In the fifty-three years between Pike's questionable treaty and statehood, Dakota and Ojibwe leaders reluctantly signed two treaties ceding the land that would become southern Minnesota—including Minneapolis. This reflected a shift in government policy. The Indian Removal Act of 1830 used treaties as a tool to remove Native peoples from their lands. It allowed the president to grant tribes land west of the Mississippi (occupied by other Indigenous nations, of course) in exchange for their lands within existing state borders.

As the fur industry slowed in the 1830s, traders who had opposed treaties started thinking the pacts might raise cash to settle debts they claimed Native people had accrued. Even some Native leaders felt small cessions of land might help address their struggles, especially as more European Americans came in without permission and exploited their resources. Lawrence Taliaferro, the longtime US Indian agent, was influential here. He was trying to help the Dakota get out from under the financial thumb of traders. These Indigenous leaders likely believed that by acceding to treaties, they were providing security as debts were paid. European American leaders also didn't want to expel Native people from the area because their annual treaty payments, made in cash, fueled the local economy.

But problems arose almost immediately. Promised payments either included useless materials, like handkerchiefs, or were canceled altogether with no warning. Fur traders saw no such delays in getting their money.

Treaties signed in 1837 and 1851 ceded all remaining land in the future Twin Cities and most of southern Minnesota—some of the best agricultural land on the planet. European American leaders had pressured the Dakota to make a deal quickly for pennies an acre, which frustrated the Dakota protocol of making such important decisions by consensus. At one gathering, territorial governor Alexander Ramsey proclaimed, "these lands have ceased to be of much value to you [Dakota], from the rapid disappearance of the game, they have become more valuable to [the president's] white children." The Dakota were left with small strips of land along the Minnesota River, and Ramsey didn't stop European Americans from moving into southern Minnesota—even before Congress ratified the treaties. Many of today's southern Minnesota cities and towns were created at this time. And in 1858, a month after Minnesota became a state, Dakota leaders were forced to sign yet another treaty that took their strip of land north of the Minnesota River.

The 1862 Homestead Act offered millions of acres throughout the United States to settler-colonists. It brought seventy-five thousand people to Minnesota in just three years, many to the areas ceded in the 1851 and 1858 treaties. The communities springing up were becoming part of Minneapolis's trade area, fueling the city's growth.

In the span of twenty-five years, the Dakota had lost most of their land. Being confined to such a small stretch of land meant they couldn't live off the land as they had for generations. They were starving and dying because crops failed and food and supplies promised them in the treaties came late or not at all. A warehouse on the Lower Sioux Agency—near the present-day town of Morton—held food that was due to them under the treaties, but when Dakota men asked for it in the summer of 1862, they were rebuffed. A trader at the agency, Andrew Myrick, reportedly responded that if the men were so hungry, they could "eat grass or their own dung." Starving and seeing their way of life destroyed, a small group of Dakota reacted violently. Four Dakota hunters killed five European Americans in Meeker County. After the hunters reported back to their leaders, the Dakota weren't unanimous about whether to go to war, but a six-week war nonetheless began. Dakota men attacked agencies, homesteads, Fort Ridgely, and New Ulm. Myrick, the shopkeeper, was killed—grass stuffed in his mouth.

Panic spread among settler-colonists with every report of a European American killed. On August 20, a headline in the *Goodhue Volunteer* in Red Wing read "Indian Troubles." "The Indians number about four thousand," the article reported, "and have become incensed either at the delay in receiving their pay, or at a supposed swindle by the agent. They have been stealing, plundering, robbing, and murdering." Soldiers were dispatched from Fort Snelling. An estimated six hundred settler-colonists and US soldiers were killed; an unknown number of Dakota died.

Governor Ramsey soon called for swift retaliation. In a special session of the legislature on September 9, 1862, he said, "The Sioux Indians of

Minnesota must be exterminated or driven forever beyond the borders of the State. . . . If any shall escape extinction, the wretched remnant must be driven beyond our borders and our frontier garrisoned with a force sufficient to forever prevent their return." In time, the Dakota were rounded up, even those who hadn't fought. A military commission with questionable legal authority tried nearly four hundred Dakota men—in a language they didn't understand, some in five minutes—and sentenced 303 to death.

Their families—some sixteen hundred people, mostly women, children, and the elderly—were moved to Fort Snelling. Most walked, sometimes encountering hostile European Americans along the way. A Dakota woman's baby was thrown to the ground; the child soon died. Dakota families to this day tell of a soldier who stabbed an elderly woman on the march; her body was never found.

Dakota people were returning to Bdote, but not for ceremony. They were eventually put into a wooden stockade, just steps from their sacred creation place.

Conditions there were crowded and muddy, until everything froze. Several hundred Dakota people died in the winter of 1862–63, mostly of measles and other diseases. "It is a very sad place now," wrote missionary Stephen Riggs. One prisoner, Wiçaḣpi Waste Wiŋ (Good Star Woman), recalled that "sometimes 20 to 50 died in a day and were buried in a long trench, the old large people underneath and the children on top." The US Holocaust Memorial Museum defines a concentration camp as a "camp in which people are detained or confined, usually under harsh conditions and without regard to legal norms of arrest and imprisonment that are acceptable in a constitutional democracy." It's a term people are hesitant to use, given its association with Nazi history. But the Nazis had *death* and *forced labor* camps, not just *concentration* camps. Fort Snelling wasn't a death camp, but it was, according to this definition, a concentration camp.

Businessman Franklin Steele, who had bought Fort Snelling after its pre–Civil War closure, opened a store in the camp. He sold food and supplies to those who could pay, thus reaping a bonanza in scrip

Dakota families held within the stockade at Fort Snelling, winter, 1862–63.
Photo by Benjamin F. Upton, MNHS Collections

(certificates entitling their bearers to land) that prisoners of mixed race
had gained in the 1851 treaty. Tourists and photographers also were
allowed in to gawk.

As this happened, President Lincoln studied the convictions of the
303 men held in Mankato, searching to differentiate between Dakota
soldiers convicted for rape or murder of civilians, and those who had
only participated in battles against US forces. He approved the execution of thirty-eight men for their roles in the war. On the day after
Christmas in 1862, all were hanged—the largest mass execution in US
history.

The *Minneapolis State Atlas* joined those calling for removal of the
Dakota, making the city's economic argument: "If the Indians are not
removed beyond the limits of the State, many of the Counties lying
along our western border will be depopulated. Thus one of the finest

agricultural regions in the Northwest, now partially developed, will be suffered to relapse into a wilderness. Can the people of this State afford to permit this vast region to be lost?"

By spring, Congress had voided all treaties with the Dakota, and the federal government arranged for the removal of all imprisoned Dakota from Minnesota. The Ho-Chunk people—who weren't involved in the war but had a parcel of good agricultural land in southern Minnesota that European American settler-colonists wanted—were expelled as well. In May, the prisoners at the Fort Snelling camp were put aboard steamers and taken to a far-off reservation west of Minnesota, in Dakota Territory.

The military in western Minnesota put a bounty out for scalps, part of an effort to enlist people's help in killing off all remaining Dakota. Soldiers then took the war to the Dakota Territory; this began the Plains Indian Wars that led to the Wounded Knee Massacre thirty years later.

In November 1865, two Dakota leaders who had escaped to Canada were hanged outside Fort Snelling. One of them, Šakpedaŋ, reportedly noted in his final words, "As the white man comes in, the Indian goes out." The Dakota Removal Act, the federal law banishing the Dakota from Minnesota, has never been repealed.

CHAPTER 2

St. Anthony Falls

If our woolly mammoths mentioned in the first chapter had, in fact, gathered along the future Hennepin Avenue and moseyed over to the newly forming river for a view, the panorama would have been strikingly different. There would *not* be any waterfall. The St. Anthony Falls that today are a hallmark of downtown Minneapolis were then pouring over a cliff in what is now downtown St. Paul.

This was twelve thousand years ago, long before St. Paul was a glimmer in a pig's eye. As glaciers retreated, their meltwater formed Glacial Lake Agassiz, a vast inland ocean. In an enormous flood, the lake drained for a couple of millennia through what is now the Minnesota River Valley. The much smaller Mississippi River drained a swampy area to the east. As the waters from both rivers flowed into future downtown St. Paul, they came upon a waterfall a half-mile across with a drop equal to the height of a sixteen- or seventeen-story building. This waterfall was roughly the size of present-day Horseshoe Falls, the largest of the Niagara Falls.

After dropping over the falls, the water bounced back and ate away at the soft sandstone that sat under the limestone riverbed above. This erosion caused the waterfall to constantly collapse in chunks. In effect, the falls spent millennia backing up to Minneapolis, losing height and width along the way. (A waterfall also moved up the Minnesota River after passing Bdote, but it met the end of the limestone, collapsed into rapids, and eventually evened out.)

These falls would one day be the source of power for major industries in Minneapolis. In making the trip upstream, from future St. Paul to future Minneapolis, the falls also helped create the conditions for not one but two hubs. Those fifteen miles between the downtowns include the fastest descent anywhere along the river's twenty-three-hundred-plus miles; a unique gorge, more than eight miles long; and the only waterfall on the river. This geology made navigation upstream from St. Paul treacherous even on a good day, meaning most steamboats and keelboats from the south were better off docking at St. Paul.

St. Paul became the head of navigation, a commercial and transshipping center to handle goods sent up and down the river—and to and from states to the west. Minneapolis, meanwhile, would later harness the power of the waterfall and create its own industries that made their own goods. The Twin Cities.

But imagine: if those Niagara-like falls had somehow not moved, Minneapolis's famed timber and flour mills might have become St. Paul enterprises, making the capital city not just a navigation center but an industrial giant. Minneapolis might never have been, or been but a far-off suburb.

For some Indigenous peoples, the falls are sacred, home to spirits that live underneath. The same oral traditions held today were noted by the first European Americans ever known to have visited the falls, who saw Dakota people holding ceremonies there.

The falls had many names. One Dakota name was Owamniyomni, meaning "whirlpool." An Ojibwe name was Gichi-gakaabikaa, which translates to "great severed rock." It's interesting to note that the Dakota name for the falls describes the water, while the Ojibwe name refers to the chunks of rock at the bottom of the falls, always present because of the constant collapsing. However, most people now know the landmark as St. Anthony Falls, the name given to them by Father Louis Hennepin.

When Hennepin first saw the falls, they were a little more than a quarter mile downstream from their current location, below where the Stone Arch Bridge now sits. Geologically, their move upstream was a long distance to travel in such a short period of time. Minnesota and

Minneapolis were still more than a century and a half from becoming a state and a city. The construction of Fort Snelling and any mills at St. Anthony Falls also was still more than a century away, as was the ratification of the Constitution.

But at the moment Hennepin saw the whirlpool by the great severed rock, eleven British colonies already existed and the institution of slavery was in place. The American experiment—complete with its revolutionary ideas around self-government and the chapters it added to humankind's history of genocide, slavery, and occupation—was underway.

Using the Falls

The first European Americans to use the power of St. Anthony Falls were from the US Army, which built a sawmill in the early 1820s to assist with the construction of Fort Snelling. They used the timber for barracks and other government buildings. Two years later, soldiers constructed a grist mill, and the power of the falls turned wheels that ground grain—grown by the soldiers on the nearby military reservation—into flour for their bread.

Even as these first mills foreshadowed the coming industries that put the falls to work for people, the spot also was becoming an attraction as a natural landmark. Artist George Catlin, who visited in 1835, promoted the idea of the "Fashionable Tour," and wealthy tourists took him up on it. A surgeon at Fort Snelling, Nathan Jarvis, noted this increase in visitors in 1835, writing, "I should not be surpris'd that in a few years this place will become as great [a] resort as Niagra." Later, as the land around the falls first became known as the Village of St. Anthony, then Minneapolis, this tourism would become a crucial feature of the economies of the fledgling settlements. Minnesota's largest building in the mid-1850s was the Winslow House, a five-story hotel near the falls whose clientele included vacationing antebellum landowners from the South who often brought along enslaved people to serve them. Minnesota banned slavery, but Minnesotans tolerated it in order to capture tourism dollars from wealthy southern slaveholders who went north to escape the summer heat and spent desperately needed hard currency in the

Visitors to Winslow House pose on the grand front steps, 1860. *Photo by William H. Jacoby, MNHS Collections*

cash-starved local economy. Many businesses besides hotels depended on their spending.

Colonel Richard and Mary Christmas of Mississippi brought their daughter and their enslaved woman, Eliza Winston, to the area in August 1860. Soon after their arrival, abolitionist allies and Emily Grey, a free African American woman, filed a complaint charging that Winston was being "restrained of her liberty by her master." A crowd of abolitionists accompanied the sheriff to the cottage on Lake Harriet where the Christmases were staying with Winston.

Legally, Winston had no case because of the Dred Scott decision: an enslaved person was property, no matter where they were. But in practice, northern judges had been ignoring the decision. Minnesota was loyal to the Union but was siding with state law; southern tourism had been dropping. A judge soon granted Winston her freedom, though she had to be spirited away to avoid protestors. Even in a new state that banned slavery and had strong abolitionist tendencies, those who profited were ready to form mobs. Though he likely had a case for appeal, Colonel Christmas didn't fight the decision. And by the next tourism season, the Civil War had started.

But some of those tourists were seeking business opportunities, not relaxation. As the army had already proven with its mills, the falls were a prize for anyone who could harness—and monetize—their power. The key to harnessing the water was to control the land adjacent, a concept known as riparian rights. If your land touches water, you also have the right to make reasonable use of the water that flows by.

Under the practices of the United States, if land was *both* ceded by Indigenous peoples via treaty *and* not directly controlled by the government, then European American settler-colonists could stake a claim to such land through preemption. If a preemptor could show he lived there, usually by building something as small as a shanty, he would get the chance to buy the land when the government put it up for sale.

During the 1820s and 1830s, the land on the west bank of the falls was part of the military reservation, and thus controlled by the US government. This made that land technically ineligible for preemption, though there were still 157 squatters recorded on the reservation in 1837. Most of them grew crops and raised livestock that fed the soldiers. The east bank, however, had been traditionally used by both Dakota and Ojibwe peoples and still hadn't been ceded by Natives. European Americans couldn't settle there until the Treaty of 1837, when Dakota leaders ceded that land.

The new commander at Fort Snelling, Joseph Plympton, soon finagled a way to open some land around the falls to settlement. Realizing no one had ever drawn the exact boundaries of the Fort Snelling military reservation, he produced a map. He kept the west side of the river—from Bdote to future downtown Minneapolis—inside the reservation.

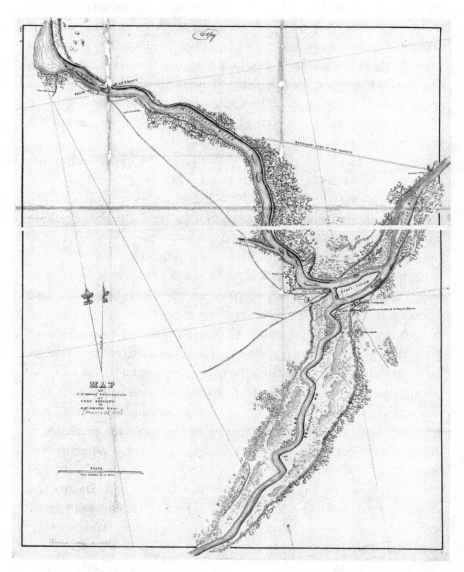

Map of the proposed Fort Snelling reservation drawn by E. K. Smith, commissioned by Major Joseph Plympton, 1838. The Falls of St. Anthony are at upper left, partially obscured by the torn paper. The reserve's northern boundary cuts to the south of the river below the falls, thus opening the east bank to preemptive claims. *MNHS Collections*

The army's mills were on the west bank at the falls, and Plympton started strongly enforcing the no-squatters rule. But the east bank at the falls was now outside the reservation. Technically, that reverted the land to Dakota control—but only until Congress ratified the pending treaty.

The Dakota who had signed the treaty protested, arguing no one should move onto the land until they were paid. They also had no say in how Plympton drew his map. But their objections were ignored. When the US Senate ratified the 1837 treaty, the race for preemptive settlement on the east bank began.

St. Anthony

In addition to being the army commander who drew the map, Plympton also was in it for himself. He was a land speculator, and he knew he would be among the first informed when word of ratification arrived. The mails traveled an arduous route from Washington, DC, in the 1830s: on steamboats down the Ohio River to the Mississippi and up to Prairie du Chien, and then carried by runners for three hundred miles along the frozen Upper Mississippi to the postmaster, who also conveniently served at Fort Snelling. That meant Plympton could get the news about ratification, then race to the east bank and build something to show preemptive ownership at the best possible spot—the falls.

But he was bested in this game by Fort Snelling's storekeeper. Franklin Steele was only twenty-five at the time, but he had his own connections to the postmaster. Upon hearing of the ratification, Steele and his accomplice raced to the east bank in the middle of the night and erected a small structure. When Plympton's party arrived the next day to claim the land, Steele offered them breakfast. Plympton still claimed land elsewhere, but Steele had taken the most desirable land, with rights to harness the falls.

Steele was now able to build the first privately owned mill at the falls; he was already part owner of another lumber mill, on the St. Croix River. But he didn't secure the financing, and the government didn't actually put the land up for sale, for another decade. Still, he gets credit for founding the milling industry at St. Anthony.

The view of St. Anthony and Minneapolis from the Winslow House, 1857, showing Main Street in St. Anthony, Hennepin Island, and "South Minneapolis." *Photo by Benjamin F. Upton, MNHS Collections*

The Village of St. Anthony, which would one day merge with Minneapolis, soon followed. The falls were the birthplace of Minneapolis.

Bde Maka Ska

About a year after the land grab at St. Anthony, another community a few miles away was bringing an experiment to an end.

A Dakota chief named Maȟpiya Wiçaṡta (Cloud Man) had founded a decade earlier an agricultural community on the shores of Bde Maka Ska (White Banks Lake), a lake within the Fort Snelling military reservation and about three and a half miles southwest of the falls. (Fort Snelling's military leaders had dubbed it Lake Calhoun, for John C. Calhoun, the secretary of war. Calhoun would later be a leading proslavery senator, arguing that slavery was a "positive good" rather than a "necessary evil.") The community, Heyate Otuŋwe (Village at the Side), was near present-day Lakewood Cemetery, just south of the Uptown neighborhood. Cloud Man had been encouraged by Lawrence Talia-ferro, the Indian agent at Fort Snelling, to move to the area. Taliaferro, who wanted to "civilize" the Dakota, also believed that if the Dakota began farming as the whites did, they would be better prepared for the time when European Americans took over their lands. (While Dakota women traditionally grew large gardens of corn, beans, and squash, they did not grow crops to sell. Dakota people shared food with relatives and others who were hungry.) And if they gave up the hunt, Christian missionaries might better work to convert them.

But Cloud Man was also influenced personally to try the colonizers' farming methods after he survived a treacherous snowstorm while hunt-ing out west. The community he founded grew corn, beans, and squash across what came to be about an eighty-acre area with about two hun-dred people. Rev. Jedediah D. Stevens opened a school on the shores of nearby Lake Harriet, the first in what would become Minneapolis; its students included children from the village. Although Taliaferro encour-aged Dakota men to do the agricultural work, women largely performed those tasks at Ḣeyate Otuŋwe, following Dakota tradition.

In 1839, the village was abandoned because Cloud Man feared the Ojibwe might retaliate for raids carried out by other Dakota people. But Cloud Man's village is an important reminder that, as St. Anthony was forming, with Minneapolis soon to follow, European Americans were in the minority. Colonel John H. Stevens, a farmer, merchant, and editor who in 1850 built the first house on the west bank of the river in what would become Minneapolis, noted that "for the first year our only neigh-bors were Indians. We have often gone to bed at night, within our home-stead, waked up in the morning and seen that while we were asleep the wigwams of either the Sioux [Dakota], Chippewa [Ojibwe], or Winne-bago [Ho-Chunk] had gone up." (Stevens's house still stands, moved to Minnehaha Park, and is open to the public.)

But a rapid change was coming for the Dakota. Bison, a traditional source of food, were disappearing from the prairie, and Cloud Man's was one of a handful of Dakota communities that had turned to farming.

And when food was scarce in the region, to the frustration of Taliaferro, Cloud Man and his people followed Dakota practice and shared the crops they harvested at Ḣeyate Otuŋwe with their relatives.

Cloud Man and his band moved to southern Minnesota after the 1851 treaty took the land he had lived on. He would return to the area where he was born, but under vastly different circumstances. In the winter of 1862–63, Cloud Man was imprisoned at the concentration camp at Fort Snelling, where he died and was buried.

CHAPTER 3

Timber, Then Flour

The workday wasn't over, but scores of storefronts stood empty. Barbers abandoned their customers mid-shave. Bakers deserted their ovens. Even doctors left their patients. Everyone, it seemed, had rushed to the banks on both sides of the river to watch the devastation.

The falls at St. Anthony were collapsing.

It was 1869. Minneapolis had been a city for just two years; St. Anthony was older, having been incorporated in 1855. The unfolding calamity could very well destroy the entire reason for both towns' existence.

Sawdust Town

The events that led to the disaster were rooted in a frenzied rush to utilize two natural resources, water and trees, to make money.

By 1869, the year of the collapse, there were eighteen mills operating at or near the falls—with eighteen different owners. The mills were there because of the waterfall, of course, but also because of the abundant forests that lay along the rivers that fed it. It is hard for twenty-first-century Minnesotans—even those who have visited or live in the north woods—to fully comprehend how thick the region used to be with trees. When European Americans started arriving en masse in the early 1800s, there were about 31.5 million acres of forests across future Minnesota. There are fewer than 18 million today, and all but a few of their valuable white pines have been logged.

Any lumberman or businessman knew a well-run and well-placed sawmill would stay in business for a long time. The first privately owned sawmill in the region was along the St. Croix River, the soon-to-be border between Minnesota and Wisconsin, at a spot called Marine on St. Croix. The lumber boom then expanded by the 1860s to the Mississippi River at St. Anthony Falls. Minneapolis soon would be a national leader in lumber production.

Everyone wanted in on the game. Franklin Steele was already part owner of the St. Croix Falls Lumber Company before his midnight land grab that let him eventually open the first mill on the east bank of the falls, at what would become the Village of St. Anthony. Three more sawmills opened in the three years following Steele's, and by 1855, the area produced twelve million board feet of timber a year.

Their success drove the desire to open the west bank of the falls (future downtown Minneapolis) to settlement. While the 1851 treaties had opened vast areas to European Americans, the military reservation on the west bank still prohibited settlement. But in 1852, Congress shrunk the size of the army's footprint.

Squatters immediately moved in—nearly three hundred of them—even though it would still be three years before the land was officially sold. Eventually, though, the squatters were allowed to buy the land where they had plopped down. By 1856, just one year after the government started selling land on the west bank, the population there had jumped to more than fifteen hundred.

A national financial panic in 1857 levied mortal damage a few miles away in St. Paul, where settler-colonists had a few years' head start on building a city. The panic halved St. Paul's population, and most businesses went under. Minneapolis fared better, largely because it was newer and had less to lose. Also, it wasn't reliant on the introduction of other commerce; the falls were creating industries from whole cloth.

With the west bank now open to settlement by European Americans, more mills quickly moved in. Illinois congressman Robert Smith persuaded the War Department to lease him the government mill, allowing him to gain the water rights. His Minneapolis Mill Company didn't initially perform any milling—instead, it built infrastructure along the river to lease to other companies. Smith and his ownership group soon added a partner from Maine, Cadwallader C. (C. C.) Washburn, who eventually became company president. From there, Washburn would move from leasing to flour milling and create what became the General Mills empire.

With lumber, flour, textile, and paper mills now on both sides of the river, companies soon joined forces to build a dam above the falls in the shape of a V to funnel water to each bank. Companies could now build mills atop the dams—in the middle of the river—and use the water flowing underneath for power. They also diverted the water inland into canals and tunnels to serve mills built there. In the years since Steele's first mill opened, humans had been substantially altering the natural appearance and flow of the falls. Now, this V-shaped dam and the system of canals and tunnels actually left the falls dry in the middle, exposing

By 1860, some sawmill owners had built mills directly over the river. *MNHS Collections*

Naming the City

Early on, the Hennepin County Board thought Albion would be a good name for the settlement west of the river at St. Anthony Falls. But a small group of men, including newspaper editor and businessman John H. Stevens, wanted a better option. They met to brainstorm. A suggestion came to merge the word "Minnehaha"—derived from the Dakota words "mni" (water) and "haha" (falls)—with the Greek word "polis" (city). During deliberations, "Minnehahapolis" was considered before the "hah" was dropped to create "Minneapolis."

the limestone riverbed to freezing and thawing in the winter and exacerbating deterioration.

The German geographer Johann Georg Kohl visited the area in 1862 and wrote about the huge buildup of walls, buildings, and dams at the falls: "The water being so low, the Mississippi could not carry away the massive load of sawdust, chips, odds and ends of board and plank, and logs dumped in upstream. This industrial waste was stuck everywhere in big jumbled heaps in the falls' attractive little niches and in rocky clefts intended by Nature for the joyous downward passage of crystalline waters. It was a miserable picture, I say." This sacred area of prayer for the Dakota, which they also believe is home to spirits that live beneath the falls, had quickly become a resource the newcomers manipulated for profits.

Given the prestige and international recognition General Mills and Pillsbury would one day have—including their easily recognizable advertising icons like Betty Crocker and Poppin' Fresh—it's easy to forget that when Minnesota became a state in 1858, flour was a fledgling industry. Construction of the first Washburn flour mill was still eight years away. The industries at the falls were national leaders in milling timber, both in output and in how many people were employed. There was no orderly transition from one burgeoning industry to the other. While timber did leave the falls first, there were decades of overlap when both industries were at the top of their game.

The boom at the falls also would influence the rest of the state, because each industry relied on material—timber and wheat—that would be grown and harvested throughout Minnesota and beyond. Minneapolis was becoming a funnel through which a major part of the rest of Minnesota's economy had to move. The funnel was St. Anthony Falls.

The Collapse

If there was a competition at this time, it wasn't between timber and flour but between west and east—the two sides of the river.

Mismanagement, debt, and a general unwillingness to cooperate hindered progress on the east side, while the west side took off. The Minneapolis Mill Company built a three-mile-long system of canals and tunnels on the west bank to allow use of waterpower at mills built away from the river. Production—and population—grew quickly. C. C. Washburn's company also began doing more than just leasing water rights. In 1866—a year after the Civil War ended, with timber still king at the falls—he built that first flour mill in Minneapolis.

Even with things languishing on the east bank, William Eastman and John Merriam wanted in. A year before the Washburns' B Mill opened, they purchased Nicollet Island, the sacred site where maple syrup had been gathered for generations and Dakota women went to give birth. After failing to get the city to buy the island for parkland, the men set forth on a plan even more ambitious than the west-bank canal.

Their purchase triggered a legal battle over water rights. The island's new owners argued that the V-shaped dam had removed the drop in the river at Nicollet Island, and thus harmed their right to its waterpower. A settlement allowed them to dig a tunnel under the falls and existing mills, from Hennepin Island, below the falls, to Nicollet Island, above them. This tunnel, called a tailrace, was a necessary and common part of mill design in the area. Water taken from the river above the falls powered turbines, then dropped into a tailrace, the off-ramp that returned it to the river below the falls.

The bottom of the Mississippi River at the falls is limestone. The tailraces were dug under that limestone, through the softer sandstone below. But residents knew that the limestone sheath ran out just twelve hundred feet above the falls. Logs thrown against the riverbed during high water wreaked enormous damage on the falls, which were also damaged by freezing and thawing. With all the additional abuse and damage to the falls caused by humans, companies started building timber aprons over the falls to preserve them. A flood destroyed one such apron in 1867; it took two tries to persuade citizens to approve a bond issue to fund another. And while Eastman and Merriam were digging their tunnel, another wet spring tore out the new apron.

After a year of digging Eastman and Merriam's tunnel, the builders had burrowed two thousand feet from Hennepin Island; another five hundred feet would get them to Nicollet Island. But on Monday, October 4, 1869, workers returning from the weekend found water leaking directly into the tunnel. Soon, it poured in. Because the sandstone was so soft, the gushing water ate away at the existing tunnel, creating a cavern. The next morning, the harder limestone above—the actual bottom of the river—collapsed, creating a huge whirlpool that sucked in everything around, including entire mills built over the falls, and spat it out the other end of the tunnel.

The news sped quickly: "The falls are going out!" Onlookers watched in horror as the calamity unfolded. While this collapse started along the east bank of the river, the entire width of the falls was in peril.

With nature already throwing "immense logs and sticks of timber about as though they were mere whitlings," as one newspaper described the collapse, what was to stop the riverbed and falls from continually eroding and collapsing? There was also a risk that Nicollet and Hennepin Islands would collapse. If the falls collapsed entirely, they would become rapids that wouldn't have the same natural power as a falls. In addition, the flow of the Mississippi might change, putting at risk businesses that relied on the existing flow. Without that waterpower, would the area's rapid growth continue?

Workers rushed to build an enormous crib, float it over the hole, and fill it with dirt and rocks. But as soon as it was in place, the river collapsed in another place. More cribs met the same fate. Plugging the holes

Destruction after the tunnel's collapse, 1869. *MNHS Collections*

wasn't working. By the end of the month, workers had built temporary dams to keep water away from the area. The fix came from the federal government, whose Army Corps of Engineers stepped in and eventually—after several years—completed the apron and secured the falls. A new wall built upstream, *under* the river, prevented water from seeping under the limestone sheath. A horseshoe dam replaced the V-shaped dam; the mills' water usage continued to dry up the riverbed above the falls during certain times of year, but the engineers built a roller dam to help maintain a pool of water in winter, thus preventing the freeze-thaw cycle. Amazingly, only one person died during the ordeal.

Eastman and Merriam nearly caused a collapse of the falls that would
have had catastrophic economic impacts throughout the young state.
But in cleaning up their mess, scientists learned important things about
the geology around the falls. And in its construction, the Corps of Engineers shored up the falls in a way that let milling continue and let the
Mississippi River continue to have its only large waterfall.

Looking west over the early stage of the wooden apron's construction, 1870.
MNHS Collections

Those fixes gave the falls the look they have today, with water in the middle. The water visitors see today in the middle of the river runs over a smooth, manufactured apron built over the actual falls to protect them from erosion. It is nothing like the place where the Dakota prayed for generations, or what Father Hennepin saw in 1680. The most important fix is one no one can see: a massive concrete wall under the river that shores up the spot where limestone ends.

The Falls of St. Anthony today are part natural, part manufactured; visitors mostly see the manufactured parts, without which there simply would be no more falls. These changes stopped the falls, after millennia, from moving farther upstream. A few articles lamented the changes but acknowledged their inevitability. Instead, the federal government—at the locals' behest—did all of this to save the area's economic engine, the mill district. The calamity mortally wounded the east bank's hopes of leadership. The fatal blow came in 1870, when an explosion set fire to several mills and crippled the east-side dam.

A detail of a bird's-eye view of Minneapolis shows the horseshoe dam above the falls, which sent much of the water into the mill ponds on either side of the river, and the low dams that maintained a year-round flow of water over the falls. *Lithograph by A. M. Smith, 1891, Library of Congress*

St. Anthony had existed first, but Minneapolis was going to be the area's hub. In 1872, three years after Eastman and Merriam's disaster, the older (St. Anthony) merged with the younger (Minneapolis). Minneapolis's growth continued thereafter at an impressive pace. By 1880, it was larger than St. Paul.

Another Collapse

Nearly 138 years later, on a humid summer evening in downtown Minneapolis, another kind of collapse happened at almost the same spot on the river. Drivers stuck in rush-hour traffic on the Interstate 35W bridge suddenly felt the bridge underneath them buckle, then collapse into the river. It was August 1, 2007, less than a mile from where the falls once nearly collapsed.

Some survivors recall the collapse as a free fall in phases, with short pauses on the way down—*boom, boom, boom.* One woman whose car sank to the river bottom has no memory of how she got out; she joked she was saved by mermaids and later got a mermaid tattoo on her arm. A group of fifty-two children and teenagers aboard a bus resting perilously against a guardrail were rescued with few physical injuries. In all, thirteen people died and 145 were injured.

The I-35W collapse became seared into the memories of a generation of Twin Citians, many of whom can recall where they were when they first heard about it. Families buried loved ones and survivors dealt with physical and emotional injuries for years afterward. The disaster resulted in heightened inspections on other bridges, an eventual financial settlement with those affected, and the construction of a nearby memorial.

But for all the trauma it caused, the I-35W collapse did not pose a long-term threat to Minneapolis. Engineers took just a few days to configure traffic detours. Commerce continued, and the rebuilding was fast, thanks to quickly approved federal funding. A new bridge opened just over a year after the collapse.

In comparison, the near collapse of the falls in 1869 threatened a two-year-old city, and the entire region, with economic ruin. The country was only four years removed from the Civil War, and investors could

The collapse of Interstate 35W bridge over the Mississippi. *Photo by Heather Munro, 2007, MNHS Collections*

have found opportunities elsewhere. Without the falls, Minneapolis had no particular advantage over other towns on the river.

Minneapolitans in both eras saw a failure of infrastructure, felt the power of natural forces, and watched the rebuilding of their community. Those who witnessed the collapse of the falls were mostly European Americans; because the Dakota had been banished six years earlier, there were few present to consider the devastation of Owamniyomni. Those killed on the bridge in 2007 included immigrants from Somalia, Cambodia, and Mexico, descendants of immigrants from Greece and Scandinavia, and a Ho-Chunk woman, perhaps a descendant of those who had been exiled from Minnesota in 1863.

CHAPTER 4

Immigration and
Corporate Growth

One of the many chores to be done on the Bohemian Flats—and one that
children could perform—was to walk the few steps to the river and
go fishing. Not for actual fish, mind you. Not for catfish, bass, or the
walleye that would one day be synonymous with angling in Minnesota.
These kids were fishing for wood.

In the years before and after Eastman and Merriam nearly destroyed
the falls, immigrants started arriving at this small patch of land at the
bottom of a bluff about a mile downriver. There they could find a plot
of land to rent for as little as fifty cents to two dollars a month. The plot
would fit a shanty and a small yard, which was often filled with gardens
and livestock. Some of the newcomers who chose to purchase instead of
rent were bilked, paying speculators a few hundred dollars for a lot that
didn't exist. They improvised, filling in the land with mud dredged from
the river bottom and chips from nearby limestone quarries.

The constant flow of refuse from the upriver timber industry kept
the wood fishers busy. People used the pieces to build rude homes
and, later, sold the wood. Oranges and bananas dumped upriver also
were plucked out of the water and eaten. But the river didn't yield just
timber flotsam; it also carried human waste. Minneapolis reported fifteen hundred cases of typhoid in 1897 alone, and these flats occupied by
immigrants were a hot spot.

The area was initially called Danish Flats, named after immigrants
from Denmark who were part of an immigration wave that lasted through

the 1860s and drew mostly northern Europeans—Danes, Swedes, and Germans. By the 1880s and 1890s, this area was largely inhabited by Czech and Slovak immigrants (with a few Connemaras from Ireland) and was given a new name that stuck: Bohemian Flats.

In the up-and-coming Minneapolis mill district that was already a timber giant and becoming a flour giant, immigrants living in places like Bohemian Flats were the workers. They could earn $1.50 a day in the lumberyards or $2 a day in the flour mills.

It was hard work, but for many immigrants, Minneapolis's industrial barons compared favorably to what they had experienced back home. Cheap housing and a strong community (there would soon be two breweries and a church at the flats) begat immigrants' common decisions to send for families.

At the top of the bluff across the river from the flats was a tony neighbor, the University of Minnesota. The institution had first opened in

Bohemian Flats in a flood, 1910, and the Washington Avenue Bridge. *Photo by George E. Luxton, MNHS Collections*

1851 as a college preparatory school just a few blocks from the falls, but it closed after the Panic of 1857. With financial support from regent John S. Pillsbury (uncle of Charles and cofounder of C. A. Pillsbury and Co.), the school reopened in 1867 on the current site of the east bank campus and reorganized as a university. It had eight faculty members and one hundred students. Even though they were just a mile from the mills, the university's first president, William Watts Folwell, noted the Old Main building stood "in a distant suburb."

Baby Minneapolis

People started locating at Bohemian Flats around the same time Minneapolis was getting its start—after several do-overs.

Back in 1855, the territorial legislature created the City of St. Anthony—the settlement of settler-colonists on the east bank of the river. Its first mayor was Henry T. Welles, a Democrat who would one day run for governor. A year later, the Town of Minneapolis was approved on the west bank. The initial council had as its first president Welles, who had moved across the river. His name does not appear on any list of Minneapolis mayors because he was technically the leader of two entities that existed only briefly.

But the legislature had erred in calling Minneapolis a town while St. Anthony had been founded as a city. If for no other reason than pride, voters rejected a referendum to proceed with the Town of Minneapolis. By law, that meant the area went back to being a township until 1866, when territorial lawmakers incorporated the City of Minneapolis. However, that law also failed in a public referendum, because its boundaries included St. Anthony.

Another do-over was needed.

The next year, a law incorporated Minneapolis as a city, this time without any of St. Anthony's land included. An election wrote Republican and sawmill-owner Dorilus Morrison into the books as Minneapolis's first mayor.

Finally.

Except not.

A few years later, in 1872, after the falls' near collapse, legislators passed yet another bill creating Minneapolis by merging the cities of Minneapolis and St. Anthony.

Making Tracks

In the mid-1850s, as Minneapolis became a hub for making things, manufacturers needed a way to get products out to far-off markets. Minnesota wanted to be part of a nationwide railroad boom. This need for railroads was also a driving force behind statehood: federal land grants were made only to states, and state governments were the entities that granted railroad charters. In 1858, its year of statehood, Minnesota had just one mile of railroad track. In the following decade, more than seven hundred miles were built.

This railroad network centered on St. Paul, the hub of navigation and commerce, with spurs off the main lines laid to Minneapolis and St. Anthony. After Minnesota's first active railroad—the Minnesota and

The Stone Arch Bridge, built to carry passengers through Minneapolis, 1900.
MNHS Collections

Pacific—went bankrupt, it was reorganized as the St. Paul & Pacific Railroad. That new company built a ten-mile line to St. Anthony in 1862.

A group led by steamboat magnate James J. Hill later bought the railroad, which eventually took the name Great Northern Railway. In 1889 the company completed a privately funded, transcontinental railroad from St. Paul to Seattle. It carried timber milled at the falls and goods shipped up the Mississippi to communities across the northern states, and it is still used today as Amtrak's Empire Builder line.

The Great Northern was based in St. Paul, but Hill left an indelible mark on Minneapolis in 1881 when he commissioned a stone bridge across the Mississippi. Initially derided as "Hill's Folly," the Stone Arch Bridge became a crucial passenger railroad link for Minneapolis, carrying passenger trains until 1978. It is now an iconic pedestrian pathway and a popular place to view the falls and the city's skyline.

Flour's Dominance

The lumber industry remained the city's largest employer for years; from 1870 to 1880, the annual value of its timber products grew from $1.73 million to $2.74 million.

Logging would continue, but new technology meant a mill didn't need a rushing waterfall for power. With new circular saws and steam power created by burning wood scraps, sawmills could be located away from waterfalls and closer to the forests that were being felled. The Mississippi River was still useful for moving logs, but at the falls, Washburn's Minneapolis Mill Company wanted to make more room for flour mills. As a result, by 1889 most sawmills had relocated to north Minneapolis, where they also had more yard space. The city would retain its title as sawmilling capital for another decade, but the era of sawmills at the falls was ending. By 1921 Minnesota's forests were gone, and the lumber industry had moved west.

Washburn wanted more flour mills because farmers in Minnesota were growing more wheat. Railroads, wheat farming, and flour milling grew together: as railroads were built across the states, farms were established that used the rails to carry their wheat to Minneapolis mills. The 1860s saw an eightfold increase in production throughout the state;

The Gopher State?

Minnesota is known as the Gopher State because of a political cartoon from the time of its statehood. Unfortunately, the gopher nickname is a case of mistaken identity.

In late 1857, Minnesota voters—that is, white males and males "of a mixture of white and Indian blood and who shall have adopted the habits and customs of civilized men"—approved a new state constitution. The first legislature immediately set up a referendum for $5 million in loans to railroad companies to build lines in Minnesota. Voters overwhelmingly approved the loans the following April, but not without several notes of objection. Why do these rich railroad magnates need our money (around $150 million in today's dollars)? Can't they just build their lines with their own fortunes?

During the debate, artist R. O. Sweeney published a cartoon showing a railroad car being pulled by nine striped rodents with human heads. The rodents represent legislators, doing the bidding of the railroad interests inside the car. A flag flying above the car reads "Gopher Train." The cartoon became popular—it went viral in an era before social media—and Minnesota's nickname soon followed.

But the rodents pulling the train car, known as striped gophers, are actually squirrels. Specifically, they are a species called the thirteen-lined ground squirrel, an animal still abundant throughout North America. Please, no one tell Goldy Gopher, the University of Minnesota's mascot.

the number doubled again in the 1870s to 34.6 million bushels. These mills used a new technology, the middlings purifier, to remove the dark (and nutritious) bran from the wheat kernel, leaving finer, whiter flour, which was wildly popular.

There were soon as many flour mills as there had been sawmills at the falls, including a six-story, limestone behemoth named the Washburn A Mill. After being a timber capital, Minneapolis was on its way to being the nation's flour capital.

R. O. Sweeney's 1857 broadside, detail.

The Minneapolis mill district, 1877. The Washburn A Mill, now the Mill City Museum, is to the left of the tracks; the Pillsbury A Mill is to the right. *MNHS Collections*

But new industry brought new danger. When wheat is ground into flour, it produces fine, very flammable flour dust. When particles of flour are suspended in air and surrounded by plenty of oxygen, it takes only a spark to ignite them. On May 2, 1878, a massive explosion— thought to be an earthquake by people who felt it in St. Paul—destroyed the Washburn A Mill. Eighteen men were killed, and the ensuing fire destroyed a third of the city's milling capacity, not to mention other businesses and homes.

The fire smoldered for a month. But much the way a new bridge would one day be quickly built to replace one that had collapsed, Washburn and other millers quickly rebuilt their mills. By 1880 there were twenty-five mills at the falls—but half of all flour produced there came from one of two companies. C. A. Pillsbury and Company and Washburn-Crosby Company owned a combined eight mills. Charles A. Pillsbury was building his empire on the east bank of the river; Washburn on the west.

Two years after the fatal Washburn A explosion, Minneapolis gained the title of the nation's largest flour producer, a distinction it would hold for fifty years. The following year, the Minneapolis Grain Exchange opened its trading floor and the new Pillsbury A Mill opened on the east bank of the river. It was the largest flour mill in the world. Flour was king.

Spy!

A month after the explosion at Washburn A Mill, an Austrian-born mechanical engineer named William De la Barre arrived in Minneapolis. He was working for a company that made dust-eliminating devices. C. C. Washburn wanted to prevent future explosions, and liked the product so much that he hired De la Barre.

In 1880, charged with helping rebuild the A Mill, De la Barre went to study milling in Europe. In Hungary, he used a disguise to gain access to a new mill, where he saw rollers instead of millstones being used to break down wheat. That borrowed—some might say stolen—technology, along with other innovations, helped Washburn's mills prosper. The eventual General Mills empire is a story written with the help of industrial espionage.

The story of Minneapolis can't be told without flour and the story of Minneapolis flour can't be told without a special mention of the year 1880. In addition to being the year the city began its fifty-year reign as flour king and the year De la Barre snagged the technology that would help it keep that crown, it was the year of the nation's only Millers' International Exhibition. The month-long exposition, in Cincinnati, saw Washburn-Crosby win several medals, including a gold for its Superlative brand of flour. By the end of that fateful year, the company had renamed the product and was selling what would become one of its most famous brands: Gold Medal Flour.

Offshoots

As a result of these burgeoning businesses, Minneapolis also became home to several offshoot industries born of the success of flour and timber.

Advertising. A robust advertising industry grew up with flour in Minneapolis, especially as competition expanded in other parts of the country. Two notables: Betty Crocker was created in 1921 to help answer customers' questions. Three years later, the company bought a struggling radio station, renamed it WCCO (after Washburn-Crosby Company), and soon broadcast a Betty Crocker radio cooking show that was an instant hit. Decades later, at General Mills' cross-river competitor, Poppin' Fresh (aka the Pillsbury Dough Boy) giggled his way into America's hearts starting in 1965.

Electricity. Entrepreneurs didn't want the falls to power only mills; they wanted to use the water to create electricity. The nation's first hydroelectric central station—the first to use water to power several buildings—opened on Upton Island near the falls in 1882 and helped light businesses along Washington Avenue. Later, De la Barre, working for the Minneapolis and St. Anthony waterpower companies, built a hydro plant below the falls that powered streetcars for Twin City Rapid Transit Company, which allowed the city to expand. Today, the plant, operated by Xcel Energy, produces about fourteen megawatts of power.

Limbs. Working in sawmills and flour mills was dangerous, as was farming and railroad work. In an era before labor unions won workplace safety rules, losing limbs wasn't uncommon. The first prosthetics companies opened in downtown Minneapolis in the 1880s and 1890s, but the need had existed since the Civil War, when so many soldiers lost legs and arms to battle and disease. The federal government helped spur the industry by offering allowances for amputee veterans to get limbs; these allowances made prosthetics affordable. Many limb makers were amputees themselves, who got into the business to improve the product. As technology developed, two ensuing world wars kept demand high. By 1918, Minneapolis was a leading prosthetics maker in the country. The Minneapolis Artificial Limb Company had one of just five government contracts to make limbs for wounded veterans during World War II, though the company would later be charged with price-fixing. Prosthetics businesses still exist across the Twin Cities today.

City Life

As Minneapolis grew, several leaders worked to make sure it had amenities like green spaces and cultural resources to prevent the city from just being a mass of buildings. Initial efforts to set aside parkland, however, were stymied by Minneapolis's small footprint, beyond which plenty of nature existed. People felt no need for parks, as the woods were so close.

Still, the state created the Minneapolis Park and Recreation Board in 1883 and businessman Charles Loring became its first president. He hired landscape architect Horace Cleveland, who had previously worked with St. Paul on its parks system.

Cleveland's master plan called for parkways that encircled the city and for parkways and parkland to encircle bodies of water, including the Mississippi River. Loring, working for years to implement the plan, eventually negotiated with waterfront landowners and developers to donate their land or exchange it for other property. It largely worked, especially around Lake Harriet, Bde Maka Ska, Lake of the Isles, and Minnehaha Creek.

Although it took decades to implement, and the city didn't follow every exact detail, Cleveland's plan exists today as the Grand Rounds Scenic Byway system. People in other parts of Minnesota own lakefront property and cabins, but very few private properties in Minneapolis are on the water.

In the same year the park board was created, a group of citizens—mostly wealthy easterners—founded the Minneapolis Society of Fine Arts. William Watts Folwell, nearing the end of his run as the University of Minnesota's first president, became the first president of this organization. The society created what became the Minneapolis Institute of Art (M.I.A., later Mia), a free museum that opened in 1915, and

An aerial view of the development emerging around Lake Harriet and Bde
Maka Ska by 1928. Rings of trees line the paths reserved for public use around
the lakes. *MNHS Collections*

the Minneapolis School of Art (later named Minneapolis College of Art
and Design, or MCAD).

The Pence Opera House, opened in 1867, was a cultural center for
the city, the first theater in what became—and still is—a robust theater
scene. The Minneapolis Symphony Orchestra was created in 1903. It
later became the Minnesota Orchestra and has given audiences across
the globe high-caliber performances (including a historic trip to Cuba
in 2015) for more than a century.

Minneapolis was slowly building its cultural pedigree, but even free
admission to many of its venues didn't make it a city with universal
access. At the time the Pence and the more prestigious Academy of Music
opened, more than a third of all people in Minneapolis, and in Minnesota, were foreign-born, mostly Scandinavians and Germans. The 1870

Women's Suffrage

The battle to extend the right to vote to women lasted for decades. The leading organization in Minnesota was the Minnesota Woman Suffrage Association (MWSA), which existed for nearly forty years before becoming a branch of the League of Women Voters in 1920.

Minnesota had passed progressive laws dealing with civil rights, including extending the vote to African American men in 1868. The women's vote, however, was more fraught. In 1870, the year the Fifteenth Amendment gave the nation's Black men the right to vote, Minnesota lawmakers approved putting a referendum to voters to let them decide whether to change the state's constitution to allow women to vote. But the governor vetoed the bill, arguing it contained illegal language. This likely was its own illegal move because only the legislature can put proposed constitutional amendments on the ballot. The governor has no say. In any case, the vote never happened.

In 1875, women won the right to vote in Minnesota, but only in elections related to schools. In April 1876, about one thousand women in Minneapolis took part in the election for school board. Charlotte Van Cleve (full name: Charlotte Ouisconsin Clark Van Cleve) and Charlotte Winchell became the first women to hold public office in Minnesota. On June 27, the *Minneapolis Tribune* expressed its general approval: "there are certainly more women than men in the community who have the leisure and the inclination to devote themselves to looking after the interest of the public schools." But the paper didn't want Minneapolis to get too carried away. "We would not favor the election of a majority of women to the [school] board," it opined. "Its important business transactions can, as a rule, be better done by men having business experience."

The quest for universal women's suffrage continued for several decades. Minneapolis hosted a national convention of the American Woman Suffrage Association (AWSA) in 1885, but further legislative efforts at the state capitol stalled.

Clara Ueland, a prominent Minneapolis women's rights activist, led a march of more than two thousand supporters through Minneapolis in 1914. The decade proved to be a time of renewed momentum for the movement. By 1919, some thirty thousand women across Minnesota belonged to local suffrage groups. The legislature that year ratified the Nineteenth Amendment; the following year, when enough states did the same, the right to vote was fully secure.

census found 4,400 of the city's 13,000 people foreign-born. The city's population also was overwhelmingly white, but social class barriers divided the wealthy from the poor.

Racial prejudice created an even harsher barrier. The 1870 census had tallied Minnesota's population at 439,000, with only 750 identified as "colored"; 109 African Americans lived in Minneapolis. It would be decades before the state's African American population surpassed one percent; most Black people in the state's early history lived in St. Paul. But Minneapolis's new entertainment venues of the 1870s found eager audiences when they booked minstrel shows that were popular among white people nationwide in the late nineteenth century. The shows featured white performers in blackface, perpetuating racist myths and lies about how Black people speak and behave that have remained to this day.

A state law in 1885 banned racial discrimination in access to public facilities, including hotels. Yet in 1910, the first racially restrictive deed was entered into the property record, mandating that no person of "Chinese, Japanese, Moorish, Turkish, Negro, Mongolian or African blood or descent" ever buy the property in question. These covenants, discussed in detail below, would become common language within real estate transactions across the city.

In 1915, the year M.I.A. opened to the masses, the first condemnations began in what became a nearly two-decades-long effort to evict all the immigrants from Bohemian Flats. The city wanted to build a barge terminal, though it was also trying to get rid of properties it deemed "slums" elsewhere in the city.

Frank Badnarek and his dog were the flats' final residents. He received an eviction notice in February 1931, but refused to leave. He hoisted a flag on his roof, even as trucks came to dump gravel ahead of new construction. Badnarek finally gave up when one load buried his doorstep. "What can a man do with all those trucks?" he lamented to newspaper reporters capturing the moment.

CHAPTER 5

Rivals!

Warrant in hand, the deputy US marshal climbed the stairs of the downtown Minneapolis office building to arrest several men. He called for backup when the group resisted and tried to slam the door on him. The glass in the door broke and cut the marshal's head before he drew his gun, telling everyone to freeze. Eventually, seven men were arrested and several bags of evidence collected. They were taken to court and arraigned before posting bond.

The war was on.

The raid in question had not broken up a gambling ring, an illegal distillery, or a brothel. Officers had arrested several businessmen, but not for racketeering or tax evasion.

The crime? Census fraud.

It was 1890, and the nation's once-a-decade census was a big deal for Minneapolis and St. Paul. In the 1880 census, after years of being the smaller (and younger) twin city, Minneapolis had eclipsed St. Paul in population by about five thousand residents. But the margin was narrow enough for St. Paul to claim that the two populations were basically equal. And there had been so much growth in both cities that the 1890 census count really was anyone's guess.

Between 1880 and 1890, both cities jumped from populations below fifty thousand to easily over one hundred thousand—a 200 percent increase. People flooding into the area were building homes on lands surrounding the cities, and leaders wanted them included in their tally. Major annexations during the 1880s drew more people into Minneapolis.

In 1883, the city—essentially a rectangle encompassing downtown and a little beyond—added a C-shaped plot that extended the borders northward, westward, and southward. Additions included the Chain of Lakes, south Minneapolis between Franklin Avenue and Thirty-Eighth Street, and north and northeast Minneapolis up to Thirty-Sixth Avenue North and Twenty-Ninth Avenue Northeast. Another annexation in 1887 expanded the city to the north, northeast, and south and gave it its final borders, save for the neighborhoods south of Fifty-Fourth Street added in 1927.

The Twin Cities' enormous growth spurt had caught the attention of the rest of the country. In his 1883 memoir *Life on the Mississippi*, Mark Twain wrote very little about the upper river, focusing mostly on the stretch from New Orleans to St. Louis. But in a satirical passage about these infant twin cities that had "sprung up in the night," Twain wrote: "When I was born St. Paul had a population of three persons; Minneapolis had just a third as many. The then population of Minneapolis died two years ago; and when he died he had seen himself undergo an increase, in forty years, of fifty-nine thousand nine hundred and ninety-nine persons. He had a frog's fertility."

Whoever had more people wouldn't win just bragging rights but also political representation (read: power) in the reapportionment to come. And in trying to get an accurate count, what was to stop a motivated group of people from fudging the numbers? Very little, it turns out. Each city levied such accusations at the other—and both were right.

The 1890 arrests sparked months of furor, vitriol, and boycotts between the cities, especially as played out in newspapers in each city (subscribers even canceled delivery of rival city papers). W. S. Daggett, the deputy marshal who had arrested the Minneapolis men, had traveled from St. Paul. Those arrested were removed by train to St. Paul for their jailing and federal courthouse appearance, where the US commissioner—an officer in the federal court system appointed to assist judges—refused to move the case back to Minneapolis.

In their time as cities, St. Paul had annexed the area between the two cities known as the Midway; Minneapolis had tried (and would keep trying) to annex communities to its west, including St. Louis Park and Hopkins, to boost its population. Despite these attempts, there had also been suggestions from newspapers and civic leaders that before too long, "the two cities will be one." The merger idea never garnered serious discussions, and never did it seem less likely than the morning after the arrests. Minneapolis political and business leaders were incensed, levying formal protests. The growing rivalry between the cities boiled over.

French humorist Léon Paul Blouet (pseudonym Max O'Rell) had noticed the tension during a lecture tour stop in St. Paul earlier that February. The two cities, he noted, "are near enough to shake hands and kiss each other, but I am afraid they avail themselves of their proximity to scratch each other's faces." The rivalry played out in daily life in serial one-upmanship. Famous lecturers and performers often had to schedule separate events in each city, as playwright Oscar Wilde did in January 1882. A bridge built across the Mississippi in 1889 connected Lake Street in Minneapolis with Marshall Avenue in St. Paul, and for generations afterward, Minneapolitans and St. Paulites have referred to the span by different names.

In 1885, when Ramsey County (home of St. Paul) donated the land its poor farm had occupied to become the permanent home of the hitherto-traveling Minnesota State Fair, Minneapolis responded by building a vast Industrial Exposition Building near St. Anthony Falls and debuting an annual industrial fair in 1886 (it lasted just a few years). Civic pride was on the line with every tit for tat.

In the end, both census tallies were dubious enough to involve Washington, DC. The superintendent of the census ordered federal agents to perform a do-over. Both cities were found to have cheated. In St. Paul, for example, enumerators—those hired to perform the counting—had tallied 275 people living (permanently!) in Union Depot and twenty-five in the barbershop of a hotel. In Minneapolis, a private detective named John H. Mason had become an enumerator and later swore in an affidavit that he had invented 122 people who were so-called family members of those on a list of names he had been given. When the

Minneapolis Exposition Building, 1938. *MNHS Collections*

dust settled, Minneapolis had 164,738 people, besting St. Paul by thirty
thousand and cementing itself as the larger twin city. Both counts were
lower than the initial totals, though Minneapolis had nearly twice as
many people who turned out to be fake (18,229) thrown out in the
recount.

Two years later Minneapolis hosted the Republican National Convention at the Industrial Exhibition Building. Minnesota, a reliable state for
Republicans at the time, was a logical choice for the convention. It came
to Minneapolis thanks in large part to the efforts of William Henry Eus-
tis, a city booster who would later become mayor. He had also helped
craft the plea deal that ended the legal fracas over the census war.

The rivalry has continued in several ways, but contemporary readers
might be surprised at how virulent the acrimony once was. Today's rib-
bing seems more good-natured than anything: early in 2019, for example, the St. Paul City Council challenged the Minneapolis council to a
snowball fight. Even then, both mayors proclaimed the event a show of
unity and the contest ended—how else?—in a tie.

Such unity is necessary in the twenty-first century, when global forces require cities to band together, think like regions, and work together as much as possible. Minneapolis and St. Paul once fought over industries like railroads. But especially in the digital age, Minneapolis's competition in the economy is as much in a capital in Asia as in the capital a few miles away.

When Major League Soccer expanded to the Twin Cities in the mid-2010s and sought a stadium, Minneapolis initially balked at public funding. St. Paul soon swept in and landed the stadium. But the debate was over public subsidies, not over the civic pride of gaining (or keeping away) another professional sports team. There's a reason most pro sports teams are named "the Minnesota _____," not "the Minneapolis _____" or "the St. Paul _____." The Vikings, Twins, and North Stars all initially located in neutral Bloomington in the 1960s, to avoid such a fight.

CHAPTER 6

The Corrupt Doc and a
Lost Reputation

It was a normal, wintery twenty-six degrees outside, with a dusting of snow to boot, but it must have been hot inside, with so many people packed into the room. The man of the hour hadn't wanted this location; he had proposed a newer building across town or even the Bijou Theater, a vast departure from tradition. But he had been overruled, so he choked out a polite speech, noting the orderly transition of things. It was the first Monday of 1901, and Minneapolis was getting a new mayor.

Albert Alonzo "Doc" Ames wasn't really a new mayor. He was being sworn in for his fourth nonconsecutive term. It was, however, his first as a Republican. The late nineteenth century was a time of Tammany-style politics in big cities, which meant a few party bosses picked candidates and doled out patronage jobs to the politically connected. In response, a progressive movement had supported direct primaries to let the people pick nominees. In this case, Ames used a good-government ideal to crawl back into office.

Doc Ames knew he would never have won the nod from either Republican or Democratic party bosses. He had started out, twenty years earlier, as a Republican, then switched to become a Democrat, and held the mayor's office three times with varying degrees of corruption. Now reformist Democrat James Gray was mayor and a lock for nomination for reelection. So in 1900, Ames switched back to the Republican Party and ran in that primary, ultimately winning the chance to take on Gray. Because the general election drew an independent candidate

Dr. Albert Alonzo Ames,
1905. *MNHS Collections*

to the race, Ames won the three-man race with less than a majority of votes.

But he hated the old city hall building where he was inaugurated. In trying to get the ceremony moved to the new city hall that was mostly (but not completely) built, Ames argued that the third floor of the old building—where the council met—would collapse under the weight of the crowd (it didn't).

The council had final say and rejected Ames's ideas, arguably his first loss as mayor. That might have been the focus of forthcoming newspaper coverage but for what happened next. That evening, Ames fired about half of the police force—more than one hundred men, those he knew were honest—and reassigned others, like the precinct captain he demoted to police station janitor. Ames had named his younger brother with questionable credentials to be police chief. A professional gambler, Norm King, was his new chief of detectives.

Doc was an actual doctor who had also attained a reputation of benevolence for giving free care to patients who couldn't afford his services. He was instrumental in the creation of the Minnesota Soldiers' Home—later named the Minnesota Veterans Home—which still operates in Minnehaha Park. But shortly before taking office, Ames used his medical office for job interviews, ultimately filling the police ranks with bartenders, saloonkeepers, and other political allies. Policing experience wasn't necessary, and the new men quickly proved the value of their alternate skills.

The new purpose of the police was to become an arm of the city's criminal underworld by monitoring—but not stopping—illegal activities. The idea was to turn a blind eye to gambling, brothels, and other swindlery; have detectives help and even direct con men; and then take a cut, passing a big chunk of it up to the mayor. Ames garnered as much as $15,000 in one year from his take on two hundred new slot machines across the city. Criminals were regularly released from jail, for a price, and there was even a scheme in which doctors' visits were forced on people in so-called disorderly homes solely to collect fees.

It was open season for organized crime in Minneapolis, but a grand jury soon started indicting Ames's men, including his brother. When the mayor was indicted in June 1902, he went to Indiana for several months and claimed he was too ill to travel back for the trial. He later resigned. While his henchmen were convicted and their sorry stories were told, Ames fled to New Hampshire to avoid arrest. Minneapolitans wondered if he would ever face justice.

Unions

At the same time Minneapolis's corrupt government was being exposed, there was growing unrest between companies and workers across several industries. The result was an increase in unionization, followed by a pushback against unions.

In 1902, a few months after Ames skipped town, a new affiliate union of the American Federation of Labor (AFL) formed. The Union of Flour and Cereal Mill Employees was the first national labor union headquartered in Minneapolis, and it soon pushed for eight-hour shifts at Washburn-Crosby mills. The company was opposed but soon granted the demand among skilled mill operatives. This labor win was significant and helped grow union membership. By 1903, nearly every flour-mill worker in Minneapolis was a union member.

When the union pressed for eight-hour days for more workers, the companies—Pillsbury and Washburn, with others—fought back. The immediate result was a flour strike that shuttered most mills in September 1903. The mills answered by hiring replacement workers and, having the money to outlast the striking workers, eventually broke the strike.

This allowed the mills to remain open shops, meaning employees weren't required to join unions. More importantly, the mill owners' success helped grow the influence and membership of a fledgling organization called the Citizens Alliance. The alliance was created in 1903 as an anti-union coalition among business owners that supported keeping Minneapolis—unlike St. Paul—an open-shop town at whatever cost. And that cost would be dear.

For Shame

The flour strike, however, was only one of Minneapolis's problems in 1903. Another happened in January, when the monthly *McClure's Magazine* published an exposé of the graft and corruption at Minneapolis city hall in an article entitled "The Shame of Minneapolis." Written by muckraker journalist Lincoln Steffens, who had spent time in the city, the story of corruption had been well documented in the local press. But Steffens showcased the saga for a national audience—a major reputation killer.

The following month, Doc Ames was arrested in New Hampshire and brought back to Minneapolis to stand trial. He was convicted and sentenced to six years of hard labor, though the Minnesota Supreme Court later overturned the conviction. Two more trials ended in mistrials, and there the case ended. Ames avoided prison and lived out his days as a doctor—still serving the masses and rarely charging patients who were poor. No man is the full caricature made of him.

Ames was convicted a few months before the flour strike. These two events laid the groundwork for what was to come. The growth of both labor unions and the anti-union Citizens Alliance set up decades of labor strife. Meanwhile, the end of Doc Ames was actually the beginning of more than forty years of corruption, as the city, like its sibling St. Paul, turned a blind eye to gangsters.

Minneapolis would live under this shame for decades. In fact, the man who would become the city's most notorious organized crime figure— Kid Cann—was just three when Ames was convicted, and the future mayor who would help turn Minneapolis in the 1940s into a "good government" example—Hubert Humphrey—was just six months old when Doc Ames died in November 1911.

How Did We Get Here?

The Ames era was a remarkable fall from grace for a city whose leaders prided themselves on being respectable. In the ensuing era of Prohibition, organized crime would wreak havoc on cities nationwide. Labor battles also would play out across the country, but perhaps nowhere as fiercely as in Minneapolis.

There are hints in the city's history about why this happened. When European Americans first occupied the land en masse, it was to make use of the economic promise of St. Anthony Falls. But power was soon concentrated among the few who could gain access to land nearest the falls and who had access to the immense sums of capital needed to develop it.

The European Americans who came to exploit the falls and Minnesota's thick forests were largely from New England. In 1860, seven years before the city was incorporated, nearly 80 percent of people in Minneapolis and St. Anthony were from the northeastern United States. They brought with them puritan ideals of common good—for instance, faith in public institutions like art museums and opera houses and favoring taxes to fund good schools and libraries.

People like John Wesley North were drawn to St. Anthony with a utopian goal of building a morally upstanding, temperate, abolitionist community—a "New England of the West." North wanted to amass a group of such fine (white) people to become "a political makeweight to . . . the dissolute, ignorant, drunken, Democratic, pro-slavery capital city down the river." Burn!

In just one year, North's letters back home helped lure about one thousand New Englanders. Their first exercise of political power was electing North a legislator. (North eventually deemed his efforts a failure, moved south, and founded a community called Northfield.)

Minneapolis's business tycoons in timber and flour, however, had national markets to consider. Historian Mary Lethert Wingerd, who makes several comparisons between the two cities in her book *Claiming the City: Politics, Faith, and the Power of Place in St. Paul,* describes Minneapolis as the place where "a small cohort of powerful capitalists—families of the original New England settlers—jealously guarded control of the city which had been the preeminent milling and manufacturing center of the Northwest. They dominated politics, finance, and business and successfully dictated the terms between business and labor. As a result of such closely held power and social exclusivity, class and ethnic tensions made Minneapolis a divided city, where claims of common civic community rang hollow."

Wingerd adds that St. Paul had been devastated by the Panic of 1857 in ways Minneapolis hadn't, forcing more compromise in its economic recovery. St. Paul became a closed shop; nearly every worker in the city was in a union. In Minneapolis, business leaders fought workers' efforts to unionize at every turn. In short, Minneapolis was an exclusive city, run by a few, powerful white men.

The Ames saga was shameful, but it played out at a time when industrial barons, familiar with the usual level of city corruption, were more concerned about unions. They focused their efforts in 1903 on building groups like the Citizens Alliance, which would prove willing to use violence to oppose unions. That doesn't mean no one cared about the city's tarnished reputation. Plenty of efforts were deployed to reform government and repair the shame. But people looking for some of the solutions to contemporary inequalities and disparities in Minneapolis can find their seeds in the first years of the twentieth century.

The Earliest Zoo

The Twin Cities today is home to two zoos, in St. Paul and in suburban Apple Valley. Minneapolis also had a small zoo in its early history, thanks to a man named Robert Jones, known as Fish.

After opening a downtown fish market in 1878, Jones started adding other living creatures to the ambiance. Fish and turtles expanded to birds and then a bear. Fish Jones would stand outside his shop on Hennepin Avenue with his bear to encourage customers to come inside.

He later sold the business and rented a home farther south on Hennepin, on land where the Basilica of St. Mary now stands. There he added more animals to what had become an informal zoo, including a lion named Hiawatha. He often paraded the animals through downtown. When the neighbors complained of smells and roars and possible mistreatment of animals, Jones moved farther south to a spot near Minnehaha Falls, in present-day Minnehaha Park. The Longfellow Zoological Gardens opened in 1907.

The zoo was popular, even with a few mishaps—a seal once escaped and swam down Minnehaha Creek to the Mississippi River before being found in Red Wing. Despite complaints from the new neighbors, Jones ran the zoo until his death in 1930. It was closed in 1937, and many of the animals were moved to Como Zoo in St. Paul.

More Seeds

By the 1910s, during an era of grandeur in city planning inspired by the City Beautiful Movement, a self-appointed group of mostly business executives called the Civic Commission had formed to reimagine a grander Minneapolis. They spent years writing, refining, and finally releasing the *Plan of Minneapolis*.

Like most cities, Minneapolis had grown using the grid model of intersecting streets. City Beautiful planners favored wide, diagonal boulevards connecting major buildings and attractions, with plazas and circles along the way. Why should avenues like the Champs-Élysées in Paris or

Minneapolis: The Capital of . . . Underwear?

Minneapolis's booming population in the late 1800s also increased the demand for warmer clothes. But the go-to ingredient for warm clothes—wool—is itchy beyond itchy. Enter George Munsing, who moved to Minneapolis in 1886 having invented a way to cover the wool with silk, making undergarments of all kinds both warm and wearable. He cofounded the Northwest Knitting Company, which later became Munsingwear.

The itchless underwear became so popular workers couldn't meet demand. But a well-timed investment from some of Minneapolis's posh residents—including flour magnate Charles Pillsbury—helped the company find its footing. Munsingwear became as synonymous with underwear as Kleenex would with tissues. Its key product early on was the union suit (think adult and kid-sized onesies that merge undershirts and long underwear).

Undercover journalist Eva McDonald went to work at the company's new factory in 1888 and published stories about the wretched working conditions, describing an unhealthy setup, low pay, and supervisors who played favorites—including one who ate the workers' lunches. Munsingwear resolved to end its sweatshop practices. By the 1900s, the company touted its worker benefits, including free, on-site medical care; Americanization classes for newly arrived immigrants; and an employee orchestra that performed during lunch breaks. These offerings were used to prevent unionization, though workers did eventually organize.

Munsingwear was the largest manufacturer of underwear in the world when it went public in 1923. For decades, it set trends in undergarment fashion and clothing. The Original Penguin clothing line came along in the 1950s and is believed to be the creator of the classic golf shirt.

Munsingwear's advertising also pushed the limits. In 1897 it was the first company to show humans modeling underwear in ads (as opposed to just images of the garments), and by the 1950s its ads sported drawings of women wearing so-called whirlpool bras and Foundette girdles. The company's famous slogan was: "Don't Say Underwear; Say Munsingwear."

The company faded, and closed its factory in 1981, a blow to its neighborhood west of downtown. The factory building now exists as the International Market Square. And with Munsingwear's donation of thousands of artifacts to the Minnesota Historical Society, the MNHS might just own the largest collection of underwear of any museum in the world.

Edgy representations of underwear in the 1920s. *Munsingwear Corporate Records, MNHS Collections*

Unter den Linden in Berlin exist only in European capitals? There was at least one practical use for wide boulevards: they might slow down fires that regularly destroyed blocks of wooden buildings across the country at the time—including a massive fire that burned twenty-three blocks of Northeast Minneapolis in 1893 that is largely forgotten today.

The National Mall in Washington, DC, was redesigned during the City Beautiful era; Philadelphia got the Parkway (later the Benjamin Franklin Parkway). St. Paul considered a boulevard running from the State Capitol to the Seven Corners area of downtown, near the present-day Xcel Energy Center. The Minneapolis plan borrowed heavily from a 1909 blueprint for Chicago and included ideas for improvements:

Extending Sixth Avenue [later, Portland Avenue] as a boulevard from
   downtown to the new Minneapolis Institute of Art and on to Lake
   Harriet. It would be a shortcut for people coming from the suburbs—
   never mind all those who would have to relocate. The plan also
   predicted "the mass of the population will live southwest of the city
   center," thus making the boulevard necessary.
Making Nicollet Island a grand park, with room for a stadium and
   maybe an airport.
Building a grand civic plaza east of downtown, near where the Vikings
   play today, that would include a municipal auditorium, a library,
   museums, schools, a courthouse, and public gardens.

The plan, which took years to finalize, was a nod to both growth and pride. Growth was easy for Minneapolitans to expect: the population had jumped an astonishing 50 percent between 1900 and 1910 (from two hundred thousand to three hundred thousand people). Where would everyone fit without thoughtful city planning? But just as important was creating civic pride, especially after the "Shame of Minneapolis" publicity. City leaders wanted to be big players, like their counterparts in New York and Chicago. Several cities were considering boulevards and grand buildings; Minneapolis didn't want to be left out.

In the end, almost none of it happened. Only four of the projects were built: the post office, the Minneapolis Institute of Art, the Gateway, and the Great Northern Depot, sometimes called Minneapolis Union Depot. The reason? In part, bad timing. After years of delays, the plan was released in September 1917, five months after the United States entered World War I.

Streetcar Strike

Labor unrest continued in Minneapolis. In 1917 the Twin City Rapid Transit Company refused to raise wages and recognize a new union of workers. The company, which ran the streetcars, had a monopoly in both cities but was based in Minneapolis (to the chagrin of St. Paul). When workers walked out, tensions boiled over in violent riots in October. Most turmoil happened in St. Paul, but Minneapolis wasn't spared. The Minnesota Home Guard, established during World War I to replace the National Guard units serving in Europe, was called in to restore order.

A significant player in the strike was the Minnesota Commission of Public Safety (MCPS), a group created by the legislature to mobilize resources during the war. It took control of many state regulatory, public safety, and military functions, using those powers to suppress and persecute immigrants and those it deemed disloyal: anyone not 100 percent American. Their targets included the Nonpartisan League (NPL), created in 1915 by farmers who banded together to fight collusion and price gouging by the grain elevators and railroads—the middlemen who brought their grain to the mills in Minneapolis.

The strike became about more than streetcar workers. On its first day, three thousand people in St. Paul attacked streetcars and shut down service. When the MCPS, acting as a moderator, backed the streetcar company in trying to break the union, the workers found their only remaining ally was the NPL. Their common enemy was the commission.

Another riot in December led to intervention from Washington, DC; President Woodrow Wilson's Mediation Commission traveled to the Twin Cities and ultimately recommended fired workers be reinstated.

The strike didn't officially end for another year, but it had a longer-lasting legacy: a coalition of the Nonpartisan League and labor that immediately fielded candidates. The marriage became the Minnesota Farmer-Labor Party, one of the most successful third parties in US history. For twenty-six years, it was the main challenger to Republicans in Minnesota. The party later merged with the Democrats in 1944 to create the Democratic-Farmer-Labor (DFL) Party.

As Minneapolis entered the Roaring Twenties, the elite class continued to exact its power in many ways—trying to clean up the city's corrupt reputation and keep workers and shared power at bay. But the conflict was still more than a decade from its peak.

CHAPTER 7

Discrimination, Redlining, and the KKK

The prejudice of the race appears to be stronger in the states which have abolished slavery than in those where it still exists; and nowhere is it so intolerant as in those states where servitude never has been known.

—Alexis de Tocqueville, *Democracy in America*, 1835

Within the first few plays of the game, the young sophomore was already hurt, his collarbone possibly broken. Football equipment back then was barely more than extra padding. But it was his first real game, and if he left, the rules meant he couldn't return until the second half. So Jack Trice (birth name John) played through the pain on October 6, 1923, as his underdog Iowa State University team played the University of Minnesota to a 7–7 tie after the first half.

Trice went down on a play during the second half. Game accounts and interviews with those who were there vary—they don't even agree on whether Trice was on offense or defense. It's not clear exactly how he was injured. Some said he put himself in danger with a move called a roll block, which was later banned. (Roll blockers essentially lunged under runners' legs to trip them up, risking an all-out trampling.) Others said that Minnesota players trampled Trice, maybe with a few kicks, to take him out. If that version has any truth, the next mystery is whether Gopher players wanted him out because he was playing so well or because Trice was the only Black player on the field.

What's not disputed is that Jack Trice was more injured than he realized when he hobbled off the field. After wincing through a painful return to Iowa, the twenty-one-year-old ended up in a hospital, developed complications, and died two days after the game.

During his memorial, the Iowa State president read from a letter Trice had written the night before the game: "My thoughts just before the first real college game of my life: The honor of my race, family + self are at stake. Everyone is expecting me to do big things. I will! My whole body + soul are to be thrown recklessly about the field tomorrow. Every time the ball is snapped, I will be trying to do more than my part." His story was rekindled in Iowa through the years; the football stadium was named after him and a statue erected on campus. Iowa State would not play the Gophers again until 1989. Today, Minnesota fans have largely forgotten their team's place in this story. And while there's no definitive proof Minnesota players targeted Trice, it's not hard to believe. Minneapolis at the time was not a friendly place for Blacks.

Jim Crow

Jim Crow seemed to be just a southern issue. After all, segregation was written into southern laws. When federal troops left the South in 1877, ending the postwar Reconstruction period, southern states reestablished racial segregation. These moves were largely validated with the 1896 Supreme Court ruling *Plessy v. Ferguson*. The decision created "separate but equal"—the tenet that segregation was fine as long as Blacks (and other nonwhite people) had their own facilities. Thus began the Jim Crow era of separate bathrooms, schools, hospitals, seats in movie theaters, and many other kinds of accommodation.

In abolitionist, Republican Minnesota—which contained, of course, some pockets of Democratic, anti-Reconstructionist sentiment—the *written* laws were more progressive. Black men could vote in Minnesota before they could nationally. Discrimination was officially banned in public places, including hotels and schools. But Blacks were still denied service in daily life. Housing on the university's campus was reserved for white students. Covenants restricted home purchases. Jack Trice could not stay with or eat with his teammates at the Radisson Hotel. In abolitionist, ethnically homogenous, Republican Minnesota, racial discrimination was still okay and thrived.

Race War

The city's elite initially built their mansions downtown. As Minneapolis grew, posh residents moved farther from the core—a common trend in cities at the time. In general, much of the working class went north and northeast as well as to near south and south-central neighborhoods, remaining close to jobs on the riverfront; the rich went farther south and southwest. Park Avenue became known as a Golden Mile with thirty-six large mansions. Another hub for the wealthy was Lowry Hill.

Later, more desirable places to live were developed near Minneapolis's southwestern lakes—Lake of the Isles, Harriet, and Bde Maka Ska (then known as Calhoun). State lawmakers created the Minneapolis Park and Recreation Board on the same day in 1883 they expanded the city's borders to include these lakes, as well as Lakes Nokomis and Hiawatha. The areas were swampy; Lake of the Isles wasn't part of early park plans because of the muck. But the well-off were quickly attracted to these spots—even Lake of the Isles, thanks to a massive dredging effort in the early 1900s.

There's a reason Minneapolis's southwest neighborhoods have always been the toniest—and the whitest: the city's white elite created some of them that way, and residents in others worked to make or keep them white.

In 1909, a Black man, Rev. William Malone, bought a home in the Linden Hills neighborhood, at 4441 Zenith Avenue South. Neighbors said that the owner, upset at them over a court case, had listed the house out of spite "for sale to negroes only." The enraged neighbors hired a Black attorney to fight the sale and prevent Malone from taking ownership. Someone shattered windows at the home, and a white minister preached, "black people should avoid going into a community where their presence is irritating." The sheriff eventually found a way to seize the house, letting the owner resell it to a neighborhood organization but not to Malone. The *Minneapolis Tribune* noted in apparent relief "the residents of Linden Hills have averted the establishment of a 'dark town' in their midst." Malone never gained the property or the chance to pass that wealth to his descendants. The house, still there today and more than a century old, was worth more than $600,000 in 2020. By 1940, the thirteen other African American residents of the Linden Hills neighborhood were gone.

This incident of racism in Linden Hills happened the same year as a "race war" in Prospect Park, a leafy neighborhood not far from the University of Minnesota. Madison and Amy Jackson bought a home there, and with their encouragement, Madison's friend and coworker William Simpson bought land on nearby Melbourne Avenue to build a house. The thought of *two* Black families was too much for neighbors, and 125 of them marched to the Jacksons' house on October 21, 1909, to read a prepared statement. "We are not here to argue," the letter read, "but to make a perfectly plain statement of our position in the matter, to wit, that we do not want you." Simpson later told a reporter he only wished to be left alone to spend his savings—about $3,400—on construction. He made no demands for social equity and didn't think any other Black families would move into the neighborhood. The Simpsons lived there into the 1920s. Their former home still stands on the property in 2020, valued at more than $350,000.

In 1910, the year following these two incidents, the first racial restriction was written into a contract for a home sold in Minneapolis. In 1917, the US Supreme Court said governments couldn't pass laws restricting property sales to certain groups of people. But covenants were written into *private* real estate contracts. The court allowed them in a 1926 ruling. Covenants would be added to tens of thousands of deeds across Hennepin County.

Minneapolis didn't need explicit Jim Crow laws like the South's to keep out Blacks. Contractual tools and other informal practices achieved the same outcomes.

Economy Down, Racism Up

Before 1910, more than 90 percent of African Americans in the United States lived in the South. This changed during the 1910s with the start

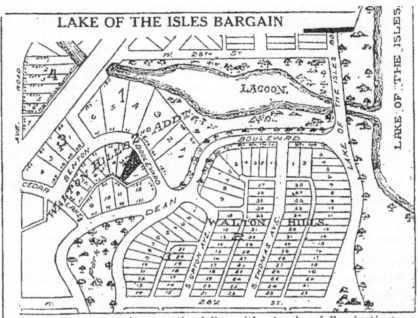

LAKE OF THE ISLES BARGAIN

A fellow cannot interest the dollar without using dollar instincts, and this lot is purposely slashed in price to attract the dollar. The map shows you where it is and what it looks at. The lot has curb and gutter, stone sidewalk, city water, gas and electricity. It is a beautiful lot, high and commanding, with a frontage of 75 feet and a depth of 140 feet. Mr. Stifft lives next door, at 2815 Benton boulevard.

Old price $4,000. Today's discount $1,250. New price **$2,750.** Terms, $750 down, balance on or before 3 years; 6% interest.

I appeal to the instincts of those about to marry. Isn't this the most remarkable offering you ever heard of. Restrictions—

The party of the second part hereby agrees that the premises hereby conveyed shall not at any time be conveyed, mortgaged or leased to any person or persons of Chinese, Japanese, Moorish, Turkish, Negro, Mongolian, Semetic or African blood or descent. Said restrictions and covenants shall run with the land and any breach of any or either thereof shall work a forfeiture of title, which may be enforced by re-entry.

Advertisement placed by Edmund G. Walton in the *Minneapolis Morning Tribune*, January 12, 1919, cheerfully asserting the value of the restricted neighborhood of the decades-long Great Migration, when some six million Blacks moved north, fleeing harsh segregation laws, domestic terrorism, forced labor, and lack of opportunity. World War I caused the first jump in the pace of movement, as the war simultaneously created new jobs in war industries and cut off the supply of new immigrant laborers.

Black migration to Minneapolis was meager in comparison to those moving to cities like Chicago and Detroit, but even these small numbers caused angst among white people. In November 1920, a meeting of two hundred residents of what is now the Kingfield neighborhood (east of Lake Harriet) protested "the presence of Negroes" in the city's southwestern-most ward (Ward Thirteen). One white attendee declared that Blacks "know they are undesirable as neighbors and hope to make a great profit on their investment by forcing white people to buy them out to get rid of them."

White people assumed that an influx of Black families had caused falling real estate prices. But that wasn't true. Prices were falling as Minneapolis entered a period of economic decline. During World War I, the city's flour mills had been crucial in feeding the country, the allies, and soldiers overseas. Production peaked in 1916, with twenty-five mills turning out 20 percent of the country's flour. This output would later help deliver on a key wartime slogan: "Food will win the war." Minneapolis's flour mills were given military security during the war to prevent sabotage. Price controls and other measures helped keep the supply of flour coming, and that continued after the war as the United States helped Europe rebuild.

But when the war efforts ended, demand for crops waned. Minnesota farmers, who had taken on debt to expand operations during the wartime boom, saw prices fall. Farmers' pain became Minneapolis's pain. Output fell at the mills. By 1930, Buffalo, New York, would replace Minneapolis as the Flour Capital of the World; its easier access to markets, transportation, and Canadian wheat gave it new advantages. Mills across the Mill City started shutting down. In some cases, the buildings were just vacated, even as the two behemoth companies— Pillsbury and General Mills, a newly incorporated company that included

Washburn-Crosby and twenty-eight other companies from across the country—remained headquartered in Minneapolis.

When people in Kingfield met to protest the presence of Black neighbors, this collapse of the flour industry was underway. But it was easier for white Minneapolitans to blame people who had different skin color (and religious beliefs) for the collapse, a phenomenon that has been repeated throughout human history.

The KKK in Minnesota

The 1915 movie *Birth of a Nation* rekindled what had been a moribund organization in the South: the Ku Klux Klan. Members of the KKK were the movie's heroes, fighting against freedmen (Blacks) and northerners in the Reconstruction South. The three-hour movie was an unprecedented hit in the young era of motion pictures. Because of the film's popularity, the KKK expanded to new places and became bolder in its public calls for white supremacy. Blacks were not the only targets; the nativist group also opposed Catholics, immigrants, and Jews—anyone who wasn't white and Protestant and born in the United States. But the film also inspired the growing civil rights movement, and there were several efforts, including some in Minneapolis, to block screenings.

The KKK organized in Minnesota in the early 1920s, its strongest years, and had at least ten chapters in Minneapolis. The North Star Klan would burn crosses on a stretch of road between Minneapolis and Robbinsdale. The Minneapolis City Council requested the police chief investigate possible Klan activity inside the police department. In response, the Klan tried to derail the reelection of Mayor George Leach in 1923 by backing Roy Miner, a high-ranking Klansman. Miner flamed out after a botched effort to defame the mayor. The Klan's backup, state senator William Campbell, could only deny that he wasn't *presently* a member. Leach won easily; Campbell won just one ward—the thirteenth, home to the same southwest neighborhoods (Linden Hills and Kingfield) where residents had protested Black neighbors.

This is the Minneapolis where Jack Trice played his final, fatal game in October 1923. The *Minnesota Daily* reported in 1923 that students

The Ku Klux Klan float that appeared in the University of Minnesota's homecoming parade, 1923 (*Myron Herbert Reynolds*), and the image that was printed in *The Gopher. MNHS Collections*

may have formed a Klan chapter on campus, though it had no definitive evidence. But the university's yearbook, *The Gopher,* carried a telling
photo taken six weeks after Trice died, at the university's 1923 homecoming parade. A car in the parade is draped in white and crafted to
look like a horse. A person stands in the car; fake leg extenders make it
look like he (or she) is riding the horse, all the while wearing a white
hood and holding a rifle. Written across the car's white cover are the
words "Ku Klux Klan."

Curious Twin

The new church that opened on Lake Street near the Mississippi River
in 1928 included a unique feature for places of worship: a broadcast
booth. Pastor Luke Rader was among the first evangelists to use the
power of radio to spread his message. It worked. As listenership grew,
so did Sunday attendance at his River Lake Gospel Tabernacle. And like
another famous radio evangelist in the 1930s, Father Charles Coughlin,
Rader's content was vitriolic: President Franklin Roosevelt's New Deal
was the "Jew Deal," part of "Satan's synagogue" that controlled the economy. These antisemitic rants were broadcast from a location in the city
that would later house the popular Longfellow Grill restaurant.

Rader also later ran for mayor and lost, but not embarrassingly—he
took 12 percent in the primary. He performed best (20 percent) in Ward
Twelve, home to his church and the Longfellow, Powderhorn, and
Nokomis neighborhoods along the river.

In addition to Rader, George Mecklenberg of Minneapolis's Wesley
Methodist Episcopal Church also preached antisemitism on the radio.
He was kicked off station WTCN after delivering a lecture called "Who
Runs Minneapolis."

It's an indication of the kind of city Minneapolis was at that time—
"the capital of anti-Semitism in the United States," according to an article
published in 1946 by prominent journalist and lecturer Carey McWilliams. With McWilliams's article, in the publication *Common Ground,*
Minneapolis's reputation got another black eye in the national press.
The piece also drew a big distinction between Minneapolis and St. Paul,

noting St. Paul's much more accepting nature. Thus, the article's title: "Minneapolis: The Curious Twin."

Historian Laura Weber, in her many writings on Minnesota's Jewish population, points out the irony of the vitriolic rants about Jews running everything. In truth, the community had to create its own organizations to help Jews find work because major corporations, banks, and government offices refused to hire them. "The hard fact remained that during the 1930s and into the 1940s, it was very difficult for Jews to get jobs in Minneapolis," Weber wrote.

Unlike other cities where immigrant Jews did factory work, options for Minneapolis Jews were to either start their own businesses or become professionals. Even then, doctors weren't given admitting privileges at hospitals (except at Minneapolis General Hospital), and some downtown office buildings limited Jewish tenants (the Yates Building accepted none).

In the period after World War I, as Minneapolis's economy started declining, discrimination increased. Economic panic has throughout history created fear and prejudice. Congress severely limited immigration with a 1924 law that set quotas on how many people would be allowed into the country. But those quotas were based on who lived in the United States in 1890, conveniently before the arrival of a wave of immigrants from southern and eastern Europe, including many Italians and Jews.

The 1924 law also maintained earlier bans on Asian immigrants and cemented the idea that those who had come before 1890 were preferred. That pre-1890 immigration was from northern Europe, including all those Scandinavians and Germans who had come to Minnesota. The law's goal was, as the US State Department's historian has written, to "preserve the ideal of US homogeneity." Until 1919, when the legislature passed a law forbidding real estate restrictions based on religion, Jews were among those included in covenants. It also didn't help in public relations terms that some of the city's most notorious underworld figures, including Kid Cann, were Jewish.

In 1936, as the city started recovering from the Great Depression, a new fascist (and antisemitic) organization called the Silver Shirts started

Kid Cann

Kid Cann, born Isadore Blumenfeld to Jewish parents in Romania, came to Minneapolis with his family in 1902, when he was two. As an impoverished kid, he turned to petty crimes, then expanded into bootlegging during Prohibition.

Because Jews were banned from jobs in so many industries, they carved out niches in the marketplace. Jewish people dominated the cigar business in Minneapolis, for example. Prohibition provided another opportunity. While there were also other prominent Jewish bootleggers in Minneapolis, Cann went further. He became a major crime figure, supplying alcohol to Al Capone's Chicago Outfit. He was arrested multiple times—including for murdering a taxicab driver in 1924 and shooting two police officers in 1928—but was never convicted. When the end of Prohibition reopened markets for retail and wholesale liquor, Cann was ready. He was the best known of the Jewish mobsters who came to control the liquor trade in the city. Under state law, a person could own only one liquor license. Cann bypassed this by having friends and family members secure licenses, moves he cemented with bribery and by having city aldermen on his payroll.

Cann continued to be investigated and indicted for various charges, but nothing ever stuck—including a charge for the murder of muckraking journalist Walter Liggett. Later, when Hubert Humphrey was elected mayor, Cann gradually moved his operations to Florida. Only in his sixties did he serve any substantial prison time, for bribing a juror.

recruiting in Minneapolis. A school board member, George Drake, was among those spotted at one of its meetings two years later.

In response to discrimination, marginalized communities formed their own groups to fight back. For Blacks, those included chapters of the National Association for the Advancement of Colored People (NAACP) and, later, the Urban League. For Jews, it was the Jewish Anti-Defamation Council of Minneapolis, founded in 1936 to investigate antisemitism (it later became the Jewish Community Relations Council). The group's own study found Minneapolis Jews were less than four percent of the city's population at the time; a majority (70 percent) lived in Near North; and most were eastern European or native-born.

Antisemitism showed in the city's politics, as well. Farmer-Labor governor Floyd B. Olson, who was elected in 1930, had grown up in the Jewish community of Near North Minneapolis. Some of his lifelong Jewish friends became his advisors. After Olson's death in office in 1936, some of these advisors stayed on to serve his successor, Elmer Benson. In 1938 Benson survived a primary challenge from an opponent who had harped on the governor's Jewish advisors. But Benson lost the general election to Republican Harold Stassen in a race that historian Hyman Berman categorized as "the most successful use of political antisemitism in the United States." Stassen never levied any attacks directly, but his supporters had circulated antisemitic pamphlets across the state.

No Laws

The lack of any formal laws to allow discrimination—in fact, the presence of several antidiscrimination laws—shows the gap between how life is governed by laws and how life is lived in practice. It was a daily decision by real estate developers to add covenants to deeds to prevent certain people from being able to buy a house. It was a daily decision by restaurant owners to ignore laws requiring them to serve Black customers, just as it was a daily decision by Black customers to not even try to be served.

The University of Minnesota had no official policy to exclude Black students from living in the dorms, but they were regularly rejected—and even removed. One student, John Pinkett Jr., was removed from Pioneer Hall after one night in the dorm; this suggests he had been placed there without anyone knowing his race. The Phyllis Wheatley House in Near North became a boardinghouse for Black students who couldn't stay in dorms. While welcoming, it was also several miles from campus—a significant commute. In a letter to Pinkett's father, University of Minnesota president Lotus Coffman noted it was "common sense"—not any formal policy—that called for segregation: "The races

Phyllis Wheatley House, 809 Aldrich Avenue North, Minneapolis, 1931. *Photo by Norton and Peel, MNHS Collections*

have never lived together, nor have they ever sought to live together," he wrote.

In 1931, the same year Pinkett was kicked out of his dorm, a bungalow at 4600 Columbus Avenue South in the Field neighborhood of South Minneapolis caught the eye of the Lee family. The selling point was two bedrooms on one floor; perfect for Arthur, Edith, and six-year-old Mary. When neighbors discovered the Lees were Black, a routine common in cities across the country unfolded: the neighborhood association offered to buy the house for more than the Lees had paid, just to get them out. They declined. From there, over several nights, growing crowds stood outside the house to hurl threats like "Burn them out!" The mob soon reached several thousand while police largely stood by. Garbage and human excrement were thrown in the front yard. The crowds were so predictable, night after hot summer night, that enterprising vendors came to sell refreshments and ice cream.

The Lees received legal help from Lena Olive Smith, the first Black woman to be a licensed lawyer in Minnesota, and the only one until 1945. She also helped found the Minneapolis Urban League and was later the first woman to be president of the Minneapolis NAACP. In representing the Lees, Smith worked for several months to protect the family's right to stay in their home—even as the crowds returned. The family hadn't broken any laws, only a taboo.

The Lees moved into a Black neighborhood a few years later. Their home, now on the National Register of Historic Places, was valued at more than $225,000 in 2020.

Actual Laws

In time, more explicit policies came along to protect the wealth of white people and inhibit Blacks and others.

The goal of the National Housing Act of 1934 was to stem the foreclosures that hit American families in the first years of the Great Depression. The federal government, through the new Federal Housing Administration (FHA), now tried to help people buy homes. A key function of the FHA was to insure mortgages—but not every one. FHA maps of urban areas plotted the safest bets to insure mortgages; the supposedly unsafe areas were colored red. This so-called redlining drew lines around concentrations of Black families.

Inside the red lines, the FHA's underwriting guidelines advised against insuring loans, and banks followed their advice. This meant that Black families paid higher interest rates and bought homes on contract, which made it far more difficult to accumulate equity (aka wealth). This practice, which in effect subsidized segregation and white supremacy, would have a profound effect on the makeup of city and suburban neighborhoods.

This is where misguided arguments that Blacks and Jews self-segregated by moving to enclaves like that in Near North fall apart. It's far more complicated than that. Jews were kept from some neighborhoods through basic discrimination, rather than covenants, but at a time when most Jews were Orthodox, communal life required businesses and synagogues be within walking distance. They gradually moved west from where they had originally settled near downtown. African Americans, who had lived all over the city, were pushed into four enclaves between 1910 and 1940: the old south side (between East Thirty-Fourth and Forty-Sixth Streets and from Nicollet Avenue to Chicago Avenue); the near north side; what we now call Cedar Riverside; and Hiawatha. For the most part, Blacks were kept in these neighborhoods through formal government policy, just as formal government policy had forced Native Americans off the land generations before. This left Black families unable to pass equity or wealth from their homes to their descendants.

Others

Other policies targeted different people, showing that Minneapolis participated in statewide and national movements that caused harm to its citizens.

> *German immigrants.* For two years during World War I, the Minnesota Commission of Public Safety used intimidation and surveillance to look for people deemed disloyal. It came down hardest on Germans, the state's largest immigrant population and whose homeland the United States was fighting. German-language schools had to start using only English in their classrooms, and noncitizens had to register property with the state.
>
> *Mentally disabled people.* In the 1920s, a growing eugenics movement reached the halls of power in Minnesota. Eugenics was a "science" that promoted selective breeding practices to increase what some considered to be a more desirable (white) population. This included a call for the legal right to sterilize people considered "undesirable"— something the Nazis would later do. Minneapolis physician Charles Fremont Dight led the effort to pass Minnesota's law, enacted in 1925, which allowed for sterilization of "feeble-minded and insane persons" who were committed to state institutions. The first six

women were sterilized at the Faribault State Hospital in 1926. By 1930, 356 women and thirty-two men had been sterilized in Minnesota, the fourth-highest number among the twenty-four states that allowed it. The law was on the books for fifty years.

Native Americans. In the late 1800s and early 1900s, US government policy called for coercing Native Americans to assimilate with the white culture whose people had forced them off their land. To this end, the government outlawed traditional religious ceremonies for Indigenous peoples and compelled Native children to attend boarding schools, many run by Christian missionaries. Native children were sometimes ripped from their parents' arms and forced into these schools. Children were given Eurocentric names and haircuts, and made to learn English and perform labor—with harsh punishments for resisting, or for speaking Native languages. A famous mantra of the time provided the rationale: "Kill the Indian, Save the Man." Teaching Native Americans to be more like white people would supposedly give them the tools to succeed in white America—an America that had never nurtured the success of those who were not from Europe or of European descent. While no boarding schools ever existed in Minneapolis, there were sixteen across Minnesota, and the effects of unimaginable trauma from separating families and destroying culture are still playing out among the city's residents today.

The law that created the Minnesota Commission of Public Safety didn't call for Germans to be targeted; that was an effect of how the law's powers were executed. Laws on sterilization and on family separation among Indigenous peoples weren't passed by the Minneapolis City Council, but they had effects within city limits, nonetheless.

The belief that Minneapolis became a more progressive place than, say, certain cities in the South is born from the fact that no formal discrimination laws existed. However, focusing only on the absence of formal language outlawing discrimination ignores the places where prejudice was allowed by what were considered the normal practices of the day.

Black neighborhoods in north Minneapolis (the Near North and Camden neighborhoods) and white neighborhoods in southwest Minneapolis didn't just happen naturally. They were influenced by generations of formal and informal processes, carried out daily by thousands of city residents and overseen by an exclusive leadership in the city that never wanted to surrender its concentrated power. That power would become painfully clear.

CHAPTER 8

Battles

Most of the injured strikers were shot in the back while running away. The carnage included two deaths.

It wasn't the first time blood was shed in the city's decades-long labor movement, nor would it be the last. But July 20, 1934—Bloody Friday, as it came to be called—was a major turning point. The resulting funeral became a mass demonstration of at least forty thousand people. The governor declared martial law, a first for Minneapolis. In spite of this, it brought a labor victory that broke the back of a group that had for years used any means possible to keep power with the owners.

The victory was long in coming. In the days before laws protected workers who tried to organize unions or negotiate collectively, the only way for workers to be heard was through collective action, usually a strike. Strikes were fairly common in the early twentieth century, especially in Minneapolis.

But the creation of the city itself, accomplished by an elite few who held their power tightly, had portended the battle to come. For years, these men controlled city politics. Doc Ames had shown in 1900 that politics were unpredictable when party leaders didn't dictate the process. The nonpartisan primary law allowed anyone to run for a party's nomination, and an unapproved candidate might be elected. At one point in the 1910s, voters elected a socialist (and very pro-union) mayor, Thomas Van Lear. In addition, the Nonpartisan League, founded in North Dakota by former socialist organizer Arthur C. Townley in 1915, morphed into the Farmer-Labor Party in 1918. The city had two F-L mayors during the 1930s.

The business owners created other means of control. An anti-union business group called the Citizens Alliance, founded in 1903, was essentially, in the words of historian William Millikan, a "union against unions." In the following decades, the actions of the Citizens Alliance "shattered any idea that organized labor might become in the foreseeable future even a junior partner in the industrial government of Minneapolis," according to professor David Paul Nord. "In fact, the complete victory of big capital over organized labor was a haunting fear." But for all the focus by unions to organize workers in the city, the Citizens Alliance kept Minneapolis an open-shop city. That meant union membership was optional—unlike in the closed-shop city of St. Paul. Even after 1933, when the National Industrial Recovery Act gave workers the right to bargain collectively, the alliance interpreted the law as not necessarily mandating unions. In fact, the alliance helped many businesses form and run their own internal "unions." In this atmosphere, many existing unions simply worked to retain what they had, instead of expanding.

But Minneapolis Teamsters Local 574 had more ambitious goals. Several leaders, including Vincent Raymond Dunne, were also Trotskyite Communists, who hoped to spark a revolution. They had their first win in February 1934, when they organized a strike among coal-truck drivers. Dunne had been a driver himself. Though their gains were modest, truckers from other industries soon became union members. In the depths of the Great Depression, with so much already lost, the goal became clear: organize every truck driver in every industry in Minneapolis and demand standard pay and hours, a closed shop, and union recognition. The trucking companies refused, and a general strike began May 16.

Thanks to careful and smart planning, workers were able to shut down truck traffic in the city. No deliveries of needed products for stores and businesses got through. If a company tried to move trucks, legions of strikers would block them. Fighting happened often.

The Citizens Alliance responded the way it had during previous strikes. It gathered its own army—so-called special deputies, appointed to fight

alongside police. Union leaders' connection to Communism also allowed
the alliance to claim it was fighting Reds. On May 22, a thousand of
these volunteer deputies were pushed back in the market district (today
known as the Warehouse District and North Loop) by determined strikers. Violence started after someone threw a crate of tomatoes through a
window. Two "special deputies" were killed.

A tepid deal stopped the violence, but it soon broke down and another
strike was called for July 16. This time, police chief Michael Johannes
issued guns to the strikebreakers. "We are going to start moving goods,"
he told his men. "You have shotguns and you know how to use them.
When we are finished with this convoy there will be other goods to move."

On Friday, July 20, as a delivery truck escorted by police was inter-
cepted by a truck filled with strikers, police opened fire. Two men died:
Henry Ness—a striking truck driver, World War I veteran, and married
father of four—along with John Belor, an unemployed worker who was

Minneapolis truck strike violence, July 20, 1934. *MNHS Collections*

Funeral of Henry Ness in front of strike headquarters at 215 South Eighth
Street, Minneapolis, 1934. *MNHS Collections*

supporting the strike. Accounts of Ness's death vary. One puts him lying
on the ground when he was shot; another has him in a truck, on the receiving end of thirty-seven bullets. Ness's funeral drew a massive crowd,
which showed where public support was.

Governor Floyd Olson—a former prosecutor who had gone after the
KKK and who had won his office with strong union support—declared
martial law and sent in the National Guard. The strike drew national
interest, including from President Roosevelt, who visited Rochester the
following month for a ceremony honoring the Mayo brothers. Roosevelt
met with labor leaders on that trip and saw to it that the head of the
federal agency making loans to large businesses during the Depression
strongly advised the industrialists to sign on to an agreement.

It took several weeks, but the strike finally ended on August 22 with
several gains for the union, including the ability to try to unionize all

Bloody Friday Investigation

Governor Floyd Olson later ordered a public investigation into Bloody Friday, the day in 1934 when police fired at striking truckers. The commission's report noted that the truck being escorted by armed police carried only enough merchandise to fit in the back seat of a car (an inefficient way to move wholesale items) and that everyone, including the strikers, was well-informed about when the truck would move. The report continued:

> Police took direct aim at the pickets and fired to kill.
>
> Physical safety of police was at no time endangered.
>
> No weapons were in the possession of the pickets in the truck.
>
> At no time did pickets attack the police, and it was obvious that pickets came unprepared for such an attack.
>
> The truck movement in question was not a serious attempt to move merchandise, but a "plant" arranged by the police.
>
> The police department did not act as an impartial police force to enforce law and order, but rather became an agency to break the strike.
>
> Police actions have been to discredit the strike and the Truck Drivers' Union so that public sentiment would be against the strikers.

firms that employed truckers. While Local 574 lost a number of those votes, it still gained members at several firms. Many leaders of the strike were later prosecuted for trying to overthrow the government—a moment historians regard as the beginning of the red scare. The Citizens Alliance (later succeeded by the Associated Industries of Minneapolis) lost its grip on the city, and Minneapolis became a union town. The following year, Congress passed the National Labor Relations Act of 1935, codifying many of the protections unions had been demanding.

Another War

The year before the Minneapolis Teamsters' Strike, Adolf Hitler forced all of Germany's trade unions to dissolve; by 1939, his invasion of Poland had caused the start of World War II. In the two years before the

United States entered the war, there was a huge national debate about neutrality. This isolationist stance initially had strong support in Minnesota, especially among Republican members of the state's congressional delegation. In September 1939, the Minnesota State Federation of Labor was calling for a constitutional amendment that would give the power to declare war to voters (and take it from Congress).

The famed aviator and Minnesota native Charles Lindbergh—one of the most celebrated people in the country—had become one of the most controversial. He brushed off charges that he was a Nazi sympathizer as he toured the country giving speeches for an isolationist organization called America First. He spoke to about twelve thousand people in the Minneapolis Auditorium in May 1941. Almost exactly four months later, at an event in Iowa, he proclaimed "the three most important

Ira Jeffery

It's not clear whether Ira Weil Jeffery ever got the package his parents sent him for Chanukah in December 1941. He had sent one letter home and a postcard to his college fraternity brothers, but neither mentioned presents.

The morning after sending that postcard, Ensign Jeffery was killed along with ninety other sailors aboard the USS *California* in the Japanese attack on Pearl Harbor. By week's end, the twenty-three-year-old would have marked six months in the navy. Born during the final months of World War I, Ensign Jeffery became the first Jewish person, one of the first University of Minnesota graduates, and the first person from Minneapolis to die in World War II.

The battleship, which saw one of the highest casualty rates among those attacked, was later raised from the floor of the harbor, rebuilt, and deployed. Jeffery was posthumously awarded a commendation for his work to help keep ammunition moving to the ship's antiaircraft guns during the attack. A few years later, the navy named a destroyer escort after him. The USS *Ira Jeffery* was the first navy warship ever named in honor of a Jewish person.

Ensign Ira Weil Jeffery, about 1940. *Nathan and Theresa Berman Upper Midwest Jewish Archives, University of Minnesota Libraries*

groups who have been pressing this country toward war are the British, the Jewish, and the Roosevelt administration." Lindbergh's remarks further diminished his standing. Public opinion had already started moving toward intervention—even before the attack on Pearl Harbor.

On December 9, 1941, college football awarded its prize for best player in the nation. The Heisman Trophy went to the captain of the team that had won the national championship—and gone undefeated—for the second straight year: Bruce "Boo" Smith of the Minnesota Golden Gophers. In an era when college football drew overwhelmingly more attention than professional leagues, the Gophers of the 1930s were a dynasty. Starting in 1934, the team won five national championships in eight years—a nice respite for a state in the depths of the Great Depression.

Smith's election made him the first—and hitherto only—Gopher Heisman winner. He accepted his award in New York two days after Pearl Harbor. He used his speech to suggest the grit of football would see our boys through in the war to come. "If six million American youngsters like myself are able to take it and come back for more, both from a physical standpoint and that of morale," he said, "if teaching team play and cooperation and exercise to go out and fight hard for the honor of our schools, then likewise the same skills can be depended on when we have to fight to defend our country." Smith himself would enlist in the navy the following year, but only after a most valuable player (MVP) performance in a college all-star game and a trip to Hollywood to film a movie about himself called *Smith of Minnesota*.

Recruitment offices in Minneapolis stayed open around the clock in the days after Pearl Harbor to handle the stream of people who wanted to enlist. By the time Boo Smith accepted his award in New York, more than fifteen hundred in Minneapolis had already applied, though most were rejected for age or health. In less than a year, about 125,000 Minnesotans had either enlisted or been drafted.

The deadliest war in human history had lasting impacts in Minneapolis and Minnesota. The families of more than sixty-four hundred

Minnesotans buried loved ones; many thousands more welcomed home those with some kind of injury. But there were a number of other effects.

The Twin Cities became a hub for a young computer industry—Silicon Valley before Silicon Valley—because of local companies' defense contracts during and after the war. As with industries across the country, several companies converted to making war materials.

Minneapolis-Honeywell, known for making home thermostats and
headquartered in Minneapolis, developed the C-1 autopilot control
panel, which put autopilot technology inside bomber planes and
allowed more accurate targeting. The company made thirty-five
thousand of the devices during the war; they were installed in the two
B-29s that dropped atomic bombs on Japan.

Federal Cartridge Corporation, a small company in Anoka that made
hunting ammunition, got a massive $87 million contract from the
government to operate the Twin Cities Ordnance Plant (TCOP; later
the Twin Cities Army Ammunition Plant), also in the suburbs.
Thousands of workers from across the Twin Cities filled shifts day
and night to make ammunition for the war. After the war, the plant
remained open, supplying the nation's military for more than fifty
years.

Northern Pump Company switched to making antiaircraft guns for the
navy with $50 million in contracts. When its original factory in
Minneapolis was no longer sufficient, Northern Pump built a new
facility in Fridley.

While many wartime companies didn't make their home in the city, plenty of their workers did. That overall economic activity helped pull the state out of the Great Depression, though as late as 1945, *Business Week* described Minneapolis and St. Paul as the "cities the war boom forgot."

With all those men off at war, companies struggled to fill jobs. Thousands of women entered the workplace, something President Roosevelt noticed when he secretly visited the Twin Cities Ordnance Plant in September 1942. By one estimate, 60 percent of TCOP's wartime employees were women. Women also became conductors on Twin Cities streetcars for the first time, and across Minnesota, farms often became women-run operations. But there was still plenty of balking at the idea of women doing any work beyond secretarial. Cargill never hired women at its ship-building plant on the Minnesota River.

TCOP also employed about a thousand African Americans during the war, a result of FDR's Executive Order 8802 that banned racial and ethnic discrimination in hiring for companies with government and defense contracts. But this order, which also aimed to protect workers with German heritage, was not universally followed. By the summer of 1942, Black leaders in the Twin Cities claimed 95 percent of war factories still were not hiring Blacks.

One of the biggest offenders was Northern Pump Company. Just three Black construction workers were known to have worked there—out of a workforce of seventy-five hundred—and they were hired only after CEO Jack Hawley was pressured. Hawley was later heard in a speech aired on KSTP radio using the N-word *twice* to describe Blacks. He also came to be seen as a war profiteer for the $448,000 salary he drew in 1941 (which he later retroactively lowered) and the $16 million he returned to the navy under a profit-limiting law in place during the war.

Minnesota's governor, Harold Stassen, also hadn't let African Americans serve alongside white people in the state's Home Defense Force, a quasi-military entity that backfilled for National Guard members who had been activated to fight overseas. Stassen, who later resigned as governor to serve in the army, also chose not to re-create the Minnesota Commission of Public Safety that had been in place during World War I.

Daily life changed for everyone. Food was rationed; vegetables and grains were grown in "victory gardens." The Dowling Community Garden in south Minneapolis started as a victory garden. Families collected scrap metal to be made into new war goods; Minneapolis and St. Paul had a wager in late 1942 to see which city could collect more (St. Paul and Ramsey County won).

Joining the Ranks

As hundreds of thousands of men left home to fight the war, women also served in military branches, though not in combat. First Lady Eleanor Roosevelt greeted inductees into the Women's Army Corps (WAC) in Minneapolis in 1943.

In numbers that have been repeated throughout the nation's history, Native Americans in Minnesota joined at higher rates than the rest of the population. More than a thousand Ojibwe and Dakota served, of a state population around thirteen thousand. The secretary of the Minnesota Chippewa Tribe had four sons in the army. Another unnamed Dakota recruit from Prairie Island told the *Red Wing Daily Republican*: "We Indians fought for three hundred years to defend our country, and we are ready to fight again if need be." Black Minnesotans also were eager to enlist, but some were turned away at recruitment offices because of their race. Those eventually accepted in the army could serve only in segregated units. The start of a war, even one that united the nation so fervently against its foe, wasn't going to be enough to stop racial discrimination.

However, there was at least one move toward racial harmony in Minnesota. Only about fifty Japanese Americans lived in the state when Pearl Harbor was bombed. Within hours, federal agents had closed Japanese businesses, including a cafe in Minneapolis that Ed Yamakazi owned. But many neighbors took up Yamakazi's and others' cause, defending them and even convincing agents to let some businesses reopen. This treatment compared favorably to what was happening on the West Coast, where public displays of hatred were commonplace. This racism had predated Pearl Harbor and was emboldened with the attack.

Two months after declaring war, FDR signed Executive Order 9066, which authorized putting tens of thousands of Japanese citizens and Japanese Americans living along the West Coast into internment camps. But the military needed those Americans' help, because many of them spoke Japanese. Colonel Kai Rasmussen picked the Twin Cities to house the Military Intelligence Service Language School. First located at an old

Civilian Conservation Corps (CCC) camp in Savage, the MISLS moved to Fort Snelling in 1944. There, Japanese Americans and others taught and learned Japanese, Korean, and Chinese to help with translation and other intelligence work, which continued after the war when the Allies occupied Japan.

By the end of 1944, more than fourteen hundred Japanese Americans had resettled in the Twin Cities, and many families stayed after the war's end. It wasn't perfect in Minnesota—and housing discrimination would increase as more Japanese arrived—but the state fared relatively well. The relationship endured; in 1955, St. Paul established a sister-city relationship with Nagasaki, one of the two Japanese cities leveled by atomic bombs. It was the first such relationship between a US city and one in Asia.

Happy Warrior

During the five months in 1945 when the war was over in Europe but not yet in Japan, Minneapolitans went to the polls to elect a mayor. By an overwhelming majority—61 percent!—they kicked out incumbent Marvin Kline in favor of a thirty-four-year-old pharmacist-turned-political-scientist named Hubert Horatio Humphrey. It was Humphrey's first electoral win, but he wasn't new to politics. He had nearly beaten Kline two years earlier.

What's more, in 1944 he was instrumental in creating a new political party. For most of Minnesota's existence, the state's small Democratic Party had been powerful only in St. Paul; the Farmer-Labor party had seen more statewide success. But it, too, had sputtered, and the parties kept dividing the non-Republican vote. Neither could capitalize on the fact that Republicans had been mostly isolationist before the war. Republicans held eight of the state's nine congressional seats in the early 1940s—and the ninth later switched to join them.

In 1944 the Democrats and Farmer-Laborites again considered merging, and Humphrey served as liaison during their tense negotiations. He also engineered the exile of many radicals, the same people who had fought the Citizens Alliance a couple of years earlier. With the deal finally reached, the two became one (amalgamated, as they liked to say) in April 1944 in Minneapolis. The Democratic-Farmer-Labor (DFL) Party was born.

Humphrey's name was immediately floated for the 1944 DFL nomination for governor, but he declined, telling delegates he wanted to help fight the war. When he flunked his physical, he took on that second run for mayor, in 1945. His win drew from an impressive coalition he had built among business leaders, labor unions, civic groups, and veterans. His optimistic demeanor would later earn him the nickname Happy Warrior.

Japan's surrender in August ended the war a month after Humphrey took office. The city faced several postwar challenges, including a housing shortage for returning veterans. The mayor struggled to meet new housing goals, even as sections of north and northeast Minneapolis were

Minneapolis mayor Hubert H. Humphrey throws out the first pitch for the Minneapolis Millers at Nicollet Park on April 27, 1948. *Minneapolis Star and Tribune Company, MNHS Collections*

set aside with rows of emergency housing trailers and Quonset huts. Leaders also appealed to homeowners to rent rooms in their homes. One public relations slogan asked citizens point-blank, "Are you hoarding an extra room?"

Organized crime was also a major problem. FBI director J. Edgar Hoover reportedly called the city "one of the four or five worst crime spots in the country." Humphrey picked a reformist police chief to combat crime and (literally) smash illegal gambling equipment, but crime figures—including Kid Cann—still retained a hold through an entrenched and corrupt liquor-licensing scheme.

But Humphrey made his most pressing and seemingly most personal endeavors in addressing the city's blighted history on racial and religious prejudice. "Government can no longer ignore displays of bigotry, violence, and discrimination," he declared in his inauguration address. He established a Fair Employment Practices Commission, one

Minneapolis Millers and Millerettes

The Twins' arrival from Washington in 1961 marked the beginning of a major league baseball presence in the Twin Cities. But baseball had a long history in Minneapolis leading up to that year.

Several teams calling themselves the Minneapolis Millers (named for the flour mills) played in different leagues between the 1880s and 1902; that year, they became part of the American Association, where they played until 1960. They won nine league championships during their existence.

They were affiliates of the Boston Red Sox and New York (later San Francisco) Giants. As such, several future stars came through Minneapolis in their early days, including Willie Mays and Ted Williams. Williams hit a home run in his first game at the Millers' home field, Nicollet Park at Nicollet Avenue and West Thirty-First Street in south Minneapolis. He also met his first wife, Doris Soule, while in Minnesota; her father was Williams's hunting guide. Mays spent just two months with the Millers in 1951 before being called up. He started well. On May 2, the day after his debut game, Halsey Hall of the *Minneapolis Tribune* provided a gleeful report: "Willie Mays said howdy-do as bombastically as any new-comer in history. He got three hits, made a sparkling catch against the flagpole, unfurled a typical throw."

During World War II, a short-lived, professional women's baseball league briefly included a Minneapolis team, the Millerettes. The Millers still played during the war, meaning the two teams competed for fans. Because of poor attendance, and because they were located so far from other teams, the Millerettes became an exclusively traveling team before being relocated to Indiana. In all, the Millerettes played home games at Nicollet Park for only two months during 1944.

Decades later, in 1987, Kelly Candaele, the son of a Millerettes player, coproduced a documentary film about the league, called *A League of Their Own*. That title was also used for a successful fictionalized movie version in 1992.

Willie Mays as a Minneapolis Miller, 1951. *Minneapolis Star and Tribune Company, MNHS Collections*

of the nation's first. Though initially limited in success, the panel established fines and even jail time for employers who discriminated in hiring. In passing the ordinance in 1947 that created the commission, the council was for the first time banning employment discrimination in the city. The *American Jewish World*, a Twin Cities newspaper, called it "the most comprehensive and aggressive measure adopted by any city thus far in the field of human rights." The commission was created thanks to the work of another Humphrey effort: the Mayor's Council on Human Relations. It was founded in 1946, the year Carey McWilliams's article calling Minneapolis "the capital of anti-Semitism in the United States" was published. The group investigated reports of discrimination and surveyed residents for their thoughts on race relations. It oversaw educational programs and developed programs to prevent discrimination in veterans' housing and by police. This was also a turning point for Minneapolis's exclusive business leaders, who had for decades largely ignored these problems. Because they were part of Humphrey's electoral coalition, the mayor had an avenue to try to bring business along.

In the summer of 1948, Humphrey—now a candidate for US Senate—took this record on civil rights to the Democratic National Convention in Philadelphia. The party included Blacks, white liberals from the North, and white southerners who held a lot of power and who had blocked civil rights legislation in Congress for decades.

Humphrey led the charge for strong language in the party platform supporting civil rights. "There are those who say to you we are rushing this issue of civil rights," Humphrey noted in a nationally broadcast speech. "I say we are 172 years late.

"To those who say that this civil-rights program is an infringement on states' rights, I say this: The time has arrived for the Democratic Party to get out of the shadow of states' rights and walk forthrightly in the bright sunlight of human rights." His argument carried the day, narrowly. Delegates from Mississippi and Alabama walked out of the convention.

Two weeks later, President Harry Truman desegregated the military by executive order. In response, segregationist governor Strom Thurmond of South Carolina entered the presidential race, nominated by the States' Rights Democratic Party (also called the Dixiecrats). He won four southern states that fall. During the same election, Humphrey garnered 60 percent of Minnesota's vote to win a US Senate seat.

Familiar Battles, Postwar

In 1950, Minneapolis reached a pinnacle. In that year's federal census, the city's population was 521,718. It's the highest-recorded population in Minneapolis history and the only time a census put the city over the half-million mark. From there, the city's population started a decades-long decline, thanks to the postwar movement of people into the suburbs and out of the Midwest in general. Minnesota was the eighteenth most populous state in 1950; it fell to twenty-first by 2010.

It's also hard to comprehend how white the city was in 1950: an incredible 98.4 percent. Fewer than eighty-five hundred people in Minneapolis listed their race as Black, American Indian, Asian and Pacific Islander, or Other. That has gradually changed. In 2010, the census tallied Minneapolis's white population at 63.8 percent.

In April 1948, the crooner Nat King Cole—already a celebrity—came to Minneapolis for a show and was invited to a party at the Carnival

Nellie Stone Johnson

Nellie Stone Johnson was elected to the Minneapolis Library Board in June 1945 (the same day Hubert Humphrey was elected mayor). This made her the first Black person ever elected to a citywide office in Minneapolis. But this historic moment wasn't her career's keystone; it was one of many chapters for the civil rights pioneer and union activist.

Johnson had learned organizing at an early age when her father, a farmer, was active in the Nonpartisan League. She moved to Minneapolis in 1922 and finished high school through a GED program at the University of Minnesota. She began organizing workers at her jobsite, even as she took classes. She was active during the 1934 Minneapolis Teamsters' Strike, delivering food to workers from her father's farm in Pine County.

After labor-friendly federal legislation was passed in 1935, Johnson worked with men like Anthony Cassius, who organized workers at the Curtis Hotel in downtown Minneapolis. She had done the same at the Minneapolis Athletic Club, where she worked. Workers at other hotels followed suit. In addition to union work, Johnson was active in the Minneapolis NAACP and the Farmer-Labor Party; she worked to help create the merger with the Democrats to make the DFL party. She led the effort for the city's Fair Employment Practices Commission, Mayor Humphrey's initiative. Throughout her career, Johnson was often the first woman in union leadership positions as well.

She died in 2002 at age ninety-six. A school in north Minneapolis is named for her, and in 2014, lawmakers approved installing a statue of her in the Minnesota State Capitol—the first such memorial for a Black woman anywhere on the capitol grounds.

Nellie Stone Johnson, far left, seated next to Anthony Cassius at an event in his honor, about 1980. *Photo by Charles Chamblis, MNHS Collections*

Club, south of downtown on Nicollet Avenue, with his new wife, Maria. The maître d' used a racial slur when telling Cole there was no room. The club apologized the next day.

The following month, the US Supreme Court ruled the covenants that had kept so many Blacks and other nonwhite people from buying homes in many Minneapolis neighborhoods were unenforceable. But in practice, the ruling had little effect. Five years later, in 1953, Minnesota banned covenants. The state passed housing antidiscrimination laws nine years later, and the federal government followed suit in 1968.

But as historian Kirsten Delegard notes, "By the time that covenants were made illegal, the damage was already done. Covenants made it difficult for African Americans to secure stable and affordable housing, which affected the health, educational opportunities and job prospects of generations of residents." One indication of the challenge of changing hearts and minds is a 1947 report from the Governor's Interracial Commission of Minnesota that found 60 percent of white people favored segregation. In addition, 63 percent said they would *not* sell their property to a Black person, even for a higher price. As Delegard points out, these patterns of residential segregation persist today.

Displaced Persons

The war's end forced the world to also consider its failure to prevent the killing of six million Jews by the Nazis during the Holocaust. In 1939 the US Congress had rejected legislation to allow twenty thousand Jewish refugee children from Germany into the country. There were still strict quotas on how many people from certain countries could enter. Even for the more than a quarter million European Jews displaced after the war, lawmakers remained wary of opening borders.

Most of those displaced persons (DPs) moved to the new state of Israel, founded and recognized by the United States and the Soviet Union in 1948. Eventually, two hundred thousand Holocaust survivors were authorized to enter the United States, though fewer than half that number did. About thirteen hundred resettled in Minnesota with about eight hundred coming to Minneapolis. It was a time of massive mobility for Jews in the Twin Cities. In 1947, there were an estimated twenty thousand Jews in Minneapolis, about four percent of the population.

Immediately after the war, most Jews in Minneapolis (60 percent) lived on the north side and there was still poverty among many of them, especially those who had recently arrived from eastern Europe. But the historical divisions between German Jews and eastern European Jews were fading. The community started to see mobility as the children of immigrants completed school—sometimes paid for with the GI Bill—and found better jobs. By 1971, less than 10 percent of all Jews in Minneapolis were blue-collar laborers, down from almost half in 1947.

Jews had already begun migrating to western suburbs, including St. Louis Park and Golden Valley, in the postwar era, because of upward mobility and their desire to move to the suburbs like other middle-class Americans. By 1956, the north side was home to just 38 percent of Minneapolis-area Jews; a full 28 percent had moved to St. Louis Park, along with the synagogue B'nai Abraham.

Plenty of "exclusive" areas and businesses still didn't allow Jews. The Auto Club of Minneapolis (later the American Automobile Association, or AAA) denied Jews membership until 1948, and Jewish doctors were barred from practicing in Twin Cities hospitals (and at most hospitals across the country). In response, the Jewish community built a nonsectarian hospital that would admit patients from all communities—and have doctors from all communities on its medical staff. Mount Sinai opened in south Minneapolis in 1951; the governor attended the opening.

More Displaced Persons

In 1947, the same year a report found most white Minnesotans preferred segregation in housing, there was another report written about "The Indian in Minnesota." Governor Luther Youngdahl had commissioned the report and wrote in the foreword: "Within Minnesota the dominant white group might set the example by correcting wrongs done to the Indian whose forefathers were on the land before the white man came." The publication focused mostly on Minnesota's eleven tribal reservations scattered across the state. It made little mention of the urban Native American population, likely because there wasn't much of one. But there was about to be.

As Minneapolis grew more diverse in the 1950s, no group saw a larger increase than Native Americans. Their population in the city grew by nearly 400 percent, from 426 in 1950 to more than two thousand in 1960; by 1970, it would be nearly six thousand.

The reason for this increase was not exactly benevolent. The same federal government that at one time had imprisoned Dakota women and children at Fort Snelling, then expelled two entire Native nations from the state, now wanted more Indigenous people in the cities. During the 1930s, the Indian Reorganization Act (also called the Indian New Deal) had started offering tribes some degree of self-government. But after the war, the federal government changed its policy regarding Native Americans to one of termination. In short, the government wanted to terminate existing reservations and no longer recognize Indigenous sovereignty. Federal funding for social services on tribal lands—which had been promised in treaties and mandated in legislation—started drying up.

In a continued effort to force assimilation, Congress passed the Indian Relocation Act in 1956. The law assisted the goals of termination by encouraging Native people to leave reservations for urban areas, where jobs were theoretically more plentiful. The government even agreed to pay moving costs and for some job training, but it did little to fund new social services in the cities.

As former Colorado senator Ben Nighthorse Campbell, a member of the Northern Cheyenne Nation, noted in 2007, the idea was "if you can't change them, absorb them until they simply disappear into the mainstream culture. In Washington's infinite wisdom, it was decided that tribes should no longer be tribes, never mind that they had been tribes for thousands of years." Minneapolis was not among the first cities picked for this program in 1951, as it was considered too close to reservations. But the number of Indigenous residents was growing, and in 1955, services followed. By 1980, hundreds of thousands of Indigenous

Americans had moved off reservations; more Native people now live in cities than on tribal land. But the jobs weren't as plentiful as predicted, given continued discrimination in hiring. Indigenous people also report they were not permitted to join unions, which kept them from gaining promotions to higher-paying jobs that required union membership.

The relocation, though, had another effect: with Native people from many nations living together, concentrated in cities, they found new ways to pool resources and gain political power. This would prepare them for the coming years of protests.

Heart Surgery

Millions of people are alive today because their heart problems were fixed with now-routine procedures that become less invasive with every advancement. Minneapolis played a critical role in this evolution: the first successful open-heart surgery happened at the University of Minnesota in 1952.

As doctors in the postwar years looked to find ways to repair heart problems, they couldn't quite get complicated machines to properly oxygenate and pump blood for patients while surgeons operated. But the University of Minnesota was developing a reputation as a place to try innovative and experimental procedures—and Drs. John Lewis and Walton Lillehei tried something different: hypothermia. They lowered patients' body temperatures, which slowed blood flow and reduced the need for oxygen in the brain.

The two performed a successful surgery using this technique on September 2, 1952. Hypothermia, however, wouldn't work for most patients with heart defects, so Lillehei then developed another method called cross-circulation: a "donor" was hooked up to the patient to pump blood for both people. This led to another first: an open-heart operation using cross-circulation on March 26, 1954. A thirteen-month-old baby, Gregory Glidden, needed a heart defect fixed. His father was hooked up to temporarily do the pumping and oxygenating for his son. The defect was successfully fixed, but young Gregory died shortly after of pneumonia.

Lillehei continued to perform and perfect this work, becoming known as the Father of Open-Heart Surgery. He later developed the world's first artificial heart valves and also worked with an electrician to build a battery-operated machine that used electricity to regulate heartbeats. That electrician, Earl Bakken, invented the first pacemaker and went on to found Medtronic, an internationally known medical-device maker that began in a garage in Minneapolis. Lillehei also trained other surgeons, including Christiaan Barnard of South Africa, who would perform the world's first heart transplant in 1967. The first heart transplant at the University of Minnesota took place in 1978.

Lillehei's transformative work put Minneapolis and the Twin Cities on the map as a hub for medical innovation, earning the area the name "Medical Alley." Hundreds of health care and medical-device companies are located throughout the region.

Dr. Walton Lillehei.
MNHS Collections

Dylan in Minneapolis

Robert Zimmerman, the grandson of eastern European Jewish immigrants, arrived at the University of Minnesota as a freshman in September 1959.

The young man had developed a love for music growing up in the northern Minnesota town of Hibbing, playing in several bands during high school. What he soon learned about the Twin Cities music scene surprised him. "I thought the only rock and roll towns were Memphis and Shreveport," he noted later. Zimmerman also discovered an emerging folk music scene in the Dinkytown neighborhood near the university, and started calling himself Bob Dillon—and later, Dylan.

Dylan lived in an apartment above what is now the Loring Bar & Restaurant (then, a drugstore) and played at a coffeehouse called Ten O'Clock Scholar. While Dylan soon dropped out of the University of Minnesota and moved to New York, his short time in Minneapolis also was formative. He heard and learned from other musicians at the time, including the iconic group Koerner, Ray & Glover—consisting of "Spider" John Koerner, Dave "Snaker" Ray, and Tony "Little Sun" Glover, notable figures in the folk and blues revival during the 1960s.

In July 1965, Dylan famously added an electric guitar to his repertoire, as debuted at the Newport Folk Festival. This drew criticism from those who charged he had abandoned a certain expected purity of the acoustic guitar. A few months later, in November, Dylan's tour brought him back to Minneapolis for the first time since leaving. He drew nine thousand to the Minneapolis Auditorium (which stood where the Minneapolis Convention Center now stands). As with his performance at Newport, Dylan's Minneapolis show drew some boos when he switched to electric guitar for the second half of the show. But he had also become a top seller earlier that summer with the song "Like a Rolling Stone." The future Nobel laureate was already a superstar.

Dylan's time in Minneapolis also coincides with a time when the city's West Bank area was a counterculture hub. Its music legacy includes the opening in 1968 of the Electric Fetus, a music store started by four friends. The independent store, despite its lampooned and bizarre name, still exists and has survived not only massive changes in the music industry but also being clipped by a tornado in 2009.

Bob Dylan and Joan Baez at the Civil Rights March on Washington, DC, August 28, 1963. *Photo by Rowland Scherman, US Information Agency, CC by 3.0*

CHAPTER 9

Urban Not-So-Renewal

Wally Marotzke had worked there for twenty years. Now, all he could do was stand on the sidewalk in the cold and lament. It was Tuesday, December 19, 1961. The city of Minneapolis wanted to be big league— the Minnesota Vikings had just finished their first season with a forgettable 3–11 record—but what the city was doing in front of Marotzke's eyes was decidedly bush league.

He had been a custodian in the Metropolitan Building, the venerable, twelve-story structure that had stood in downtown Minneapolis for seven decades—and for a while was the city's tallest. The Met was architecturally significant, but it had ended up on the business end of a plan to raze several blocks of "blighted" buildings—all in the name of urban renewal.

Marotzke's last job, he told a reporter, was emptying the building's pipes. "I hated it," he added, because he knew he was helping bring the building to its demise. In his last weeks, he took a few mementos, but he had no plans to be there the next day, when crews showed up to start demolition. "The future generations are gonna read about this building," he said, "and they'll see some of the buildings they're putting up here and they will damn us, they will, for tearing down the Met." Indeed, the inability to save the Met, coupled with later, high-profile preservation failures like Penn Station in New York, helped establish local and nationwide tools to preserve historic buildings and neighborhoods.

Less than five months later, the Dayton family, who had long operated a celebrated department store in downtown Minneapolis, debuted

The Metropolitan Building in downtown Minneapolis, 1961. *Photo by Robert Jacobson, MNHS Collections*

Wally Marotzke takes a final look at his workplace, 1961. *Photo by Earl Seubert, MNHS Collections*

their latest enterprise in the nearby suburb of Roseville: a discount store called Target.

The Met's death and Target's birth aren't directly connected, but it's no accident they happened so close together in time.

Suburbs

The same New Deal program that created redlining—the boxing out of certain urban neighborhoods where federal backing for housing loans was routinely denied—also had helped subsidize the growth of suburbs before the war. Those developments won those subsidies only if the homes were sold to white families and included covenants that prohibited future sale to Blacks. Federal housing loans made to returning veterans followed the same practices. As the growth of suburbs took off after the war, these barriers only compounded the whiteness of new communities built outside of Minneapolis and St. Paul.

After peaking in the 1950 census, Minneapolis's population began a four-decade decline. The overall loss of eighty-seven thousand people from 1950 to 1970 masks the fact that nearly 107,000 white people left the city during that time. This had several implications: fewer residents meant a decline in property and other tax revenues. And the city could no longer grow by annexation, because it was ringed in by the suburbs.

These national trends of migration to the suburbs happened as Minneapolis's storied flour industry also was in decline. People still needed flour, but the industry's leaders no longer needed the flour mills to be in Minneapolis. By 1930, the nation's leading center for milling flour was Buffalo, New York, which was closer to eastern and international markets and well situated to process Canadian wheat. Minneapolis mills had been closing since the 1920s. Huge buildings stood vacant along the west side of the river at the falls. The canal that had been built to channel water to inland mills was filled in with gravel. The city got a civic gut punch in 1955 when General Mills, the company whose founders had built Minneapolis, moved its headquarters (along with eight hundred employees who had spent lunch hours shopping and eating downtown) to a new campus in suburban Golden Valley.

The following year, the Dayton Company opened a $20 million project located on five hundred acres of former cornfield in the southwestern suburb of Edina. Southdale Center had five thousand easily accessible parking spots and dozens of stores (including, of course, a Dayton's) and was entirely indoors and weatherproof—a first for any mall in the country.

The mall was built in part to be a place people could maneuver with relative ease in the winter months. But it was also a reality check on what businesses in Minneapolis faced in the near future; many stores in Southdale also had locations downtown. The opening gala drew seventy-five thousand; the following weekend, another 188,000.

One writer called Southdale "the Minneapolis downtown you would get if you started over and corrected all the mistakes that were made the first time around." Ouch.

Southdale Mall, Edina, 1956. *Minneapolis Star Journal Tribune, MNHS Collections*

Slum Clearance

Civic leaders wanted to make sure Minneapolis remained an economic hub, and they zeroed in on the idea that they would have to clear out and rebuild areas they deemed blighted or decayed. Calling something blighted or a ghetto or a slum usually didn't take into account the people who lived there; the city's white leaders made those calls based on what looked presentable to them and what didn't.

Minneapolis's original commercial center was Bridge Square, at the south end of the Hennepin Avenue Bridge, but businesses had long since moved farther downtown, away from the river. This area, now known as the Gateway, became the focus for clearing. Thanks to city liquor laws that dated to the 1880s, the Gateway was one of the few places where businesses could sell liquor. As such, the area became a skid row of bars, dilapidated buildings, and flophouses. Bar owners paid off police to ignore sex workers and gambling. Those who lived in the area were mostly single, including seasonal laborers when they weren't working on farms or in mills. Fearing the city was about to become "a doughnut with a hole of blight," according to the chamber of commerce, the city's political leaders decided to knock down those buildings. Yet even as a skid row, the Gateway contained architecture that preservationists later would lament had been lost.

One early idea for the Gateway was to raze everything and build a freeway through that part of downtown. That never happened, but the city eventually got enough federal funding to demolish nearly two hundred buildings in the Gateway. It was the largest urban renewal plan ever undertaken in any American downtown. The city's Housing and Redevelopment Authority (HRA) had final say on which buildings to tear down. Despite calls to save it, the HRA voted to include the Met. At one point in its past, HRA offices had been on the Met's top floor.

However, once the Gateway was flattened, city leaders found it harder to fill in. While they had met the goal to clear an area they considered blighted, about 40 percent of the Gateway district remained undeveloped a decade after clearing. In a twisted irony, the spot that formerly held the Metropolitan Building remained a parking lot until 1980—long after federal and state laws were passed to support the preservation of historic buildings.

New Lock

With the flour mills mostly closed, community leaders worked to jumpstart the city's connection to the river by finally bringing robust commercial traffic to St. Anthony Falls. St. Paul had always been the place where boats landed because navigating upriver to Minneapolis was so treacherous. But a series of modern locks would fix that. And, the thinking went, if we could just build those locks, all that commerce ceded to St. Paul since the city's early days would start coming to Minneapolis and help replace what was lost when the mills closed.

Two locks were needed—one at the falls and another downriver near the future I-35W bridge. It took from 1959 to 1963 to wedge a massive lock into the area at the falls where the mills once reigned. The construction further changed the look of the area. Most remaining milling infrastructure was removed, as were Upton Island and the remnants of Spirit Island, the island sacred to the Dakota people that had become a shell of its former self after decades of being quarried for its limestone.

At the lock's opening ceremony in 1963, Congressman Walter Judd declared, "I don't know of any public works appropriation that I voted for that will bring as many benefits as this one in 50 or 100 years." That turned out to be an oversell; the anticipated river commerce never fully manifested. By and large, as historian Iric Nathanson wrote, "the city had turned its back on the river during the decades following the milling industry's collapse." In the end, it was yet another invader that sealed the lock's fate. In June 2015, after fifty-two years in operation, the massive structure was closed to river traffic to try to block the march of invasive carp that have wreaked havoc along the Mississippi and other rivers to the south. A successor to Congressman Judd—Representative Keith Ellison—said the closure was justified, in part, because the lock was "little used."

Buildings

The rest of downtown's core also got a facelift during this time. While that brought a new look to downtown, many buildings ultimately became largely indistinguishable—with at least one notable exception.

The Beatles

In August 1965, the Beatles were at the height of their popularity when they made their second tour of the United States and Canada. The sixteen shows (in sixteen days) included a stop at Metropolitan Stadium on August 21. It was the only show that didn't sell out.

Granted, there were thirty thousand people in attendance, who had each paid between $3.50 and $5.50 for admission. But twelve thousand tickets went unsold for the Beatles' only trip to Minnesota. The Fab Four played only eleven songs over thirty-five minutes (they were one of several bands who played), and earned a cool $50,000 for their time.

At the time, showgoers at Met Stadium weren't allowed on the field, meaning the stage (near second base) was a short sprint from the nearest fan. Most recollections from attendees and news reports detail the constant screams from adoring fans and the inability to hear all the songs. "While there were large portions of the songs that you could hear over the frenzied roar," wrote Allan Holbert the next day in the *Minneapolis Tribune*, "it was impossible to tell what they were singing unless you were sitting by a teen-ager who could tell you the names of the songs." "Help!" indeed! (And yes, they played it.)

While at Met Stadium, the band had access to the Minnesota Twins' locker room, and, according to the clubhouse manager, John, Paul, George, and Ringo all took saunas for the first time. Ah, the little things in life.

The Beatles in concert at Metropolitan Stadium, Bloomington, August 21, 1965. *Photo by Sully Doroshow, St. Paul Dispatch–Pioneer Press, MNHS Collections*

Since 1929, the Foshay Tower had been Minneapolis's tallest building. The businessman who built it, Wilbur Foshay, modeled it after the
Washington Monument. Foshay lost his fortune in the stock market
crash of October 1929, the month after he opened his tower, and the
building changed owners several times. But it kept its height record until
the 1970s, when the IDS Center opened, built as the headquarters for
Investors Diversified Services, Inc. In designing the IDS, famed architect Philip Johnson gave Minneapolis fifty-five floors of glass to Foshay's
thirty-two floors of limestone.

The IDS fit well with a new pedestrian mall along Nicollet Avenue. It
was also the first major building designed to incorporate downtown's
newest feature: skyways. The covered walkways that connect buildings
at their second floors had debuted in 1962. Over the years, the skyway

The IDS Tower under
construction, 1971.
*Photo by Elmer Bloom,
MNHS Collections*

system has grown to be the world's largest. The debate over skyways has never been settled. Should we hate them for robbing a major metropolis of street life and pushing it to the second floor, separating the haves from the have-nots? Or does the climate control compete well with malls and other developments in the suburbs, helping downtown save some of what it might otherwise have lost?

Freeways

In 1956, the same year Southdale Center opened, Congress passed the Federal Aid Highway Act, launching the interstate highway system. Many cities used the funds to construct new highways designed to cut through neighborhoods they deemed blighted or ghettos, and many interested parties—city planners, historians, activists—continue to study their effects on neighborhoods and communities across the country. Interstate 94 was built to connect the Minneapolis and St. Paul downtowns. The freeway tore through the heart of the historically Black Rondo neighborhood in St. Paul, but it spared Prospect Park in Minneapolis. It probably didn't hurt that Minneapolis's mayor at the time, Art Naftalin, lived in that neighborhood.

Interstate 35W approaches the city's downtown through Northeast Minneapolis, passes the University of Minnesota, runs around the east end of downtown, and then shoots straight south through south Minneapolis. But the route jigs a little to the east just south of downtown, in order to miss barreling through the Minneapolis Institute of Art. In sparing the museum, however, the route went through a Mexican and Black neighborhood. "The freeway did a number on my childhood space," lamented Beverly Latkin, who lived in the area when the freeways were built, to the community newspaper *The Alley*. "It barreled right through the middle of a minority neighborhood. I watched the houses go down one by one." Joe Steffel, who also grew up in the neighborhood, told the paper the highway ended a sense of community; it became a de facto barrier, with Blacks to the east, white people to the west. "We were caught in the middle, weren't involved downtown or out in the suburbs. . . . You don't feel like you have any roots, you're stuck in purgatory."

I-35W taking out a swath of south Minneapolis, as seen from a helicopter.
Photo © Ray Cowdery, Hennepin History Museum

Later, in a separate part of south Minneapolis, a yearslong fight took place over whether to make Hiawatha Avenue (Highway 55) a freeway. In this case, pushback and protest from the majority-white community helped, as did several decades of experience seeing what highways did to communities. Controversies were over the exact route; whether the road should be a sunken freeway (like I-94 and I-35W) or at grade; and whether the strip should be only for cars or include some kind of mass transit, which it ultimately did.

Also, in the 1970s the city axed plans to build I-335, a freeway through the St. Anthony West neighborhood in Northeast Minneapolis. The two-mile spur would have connected I-35W to I-94 north of downtown by going through, among other places, Boom Island Park.

As happened in cities across the country, this postwar acceleration of highway construction massively and forever changed the look of Minneapolis. Neighborhoods were lost—or saved—or completely cut off from their historic neighbors. The city's history is filled with efforts to separate people—but usually in subtle or invisible ways, like racial covenants. Highway construction was a blunter tool with the same effect in some cases, especially for people who had no influence with city leaders.

CHAPTER 10

Voices Heard

The civil rights movement of the 1960s also played out in Minneapolis, where discrimination in accommodations had ended. But several picket lines outside Twin Cities' Woolworth, Kresge, and W. T. Grant stores that year raised the profile of companies that refused to serve Blacks in other states. If their parent companies still owned stores that discriminated elsewhere, the NAACP argued, the Minneapolis and St. Paul locations warranted a picket line. Local civil rights activists Josie Johnson and Matt Little were among those who attended the 1963 March on Washington for Jobs and Freedom, during which Rev. Martin Luther King Jr. gave his "I Have a Dream" speech.

The US Supreme Court had desegregated schools in 1954, but more than a decade later, Minneapolis newspapers found examples of schools with only a handful of Black students. Even with national legislative wins, including the Civil Rights Act of 1964 and the Voting Rights Act of 1965, the inequities continued—rampantly, in some cases.

Music

Into the late 1960s, an unofficial rule still existed in the live music venues of downtown Minneapolis: no bands with more than one Black member. "I don't know what caused it, but there was nobody working," recalled saxophonist Irv Williams to writer Andrea Swensson for her music history of the time, *Got to Be Something Here: The Rise of the Minneapolis Sound.* "You'd go up and down Hennepin, and you wouldn't see any

Calvin Griffith Tees Off

On September 20, 1978, near the end of a forgettable Minnesota Twins baseball season, the Lions Club in the southern Minnesota town of Waseca scored a big-ticket guest: Calvin Griffith, the team's owner. During a question-and-answer period, one Lion asked why Griffith had brought the team to Minnesota from Washington in 1961.

Partway through his answer, he paused and asked if any Blacks were in the room before continuing: "I'll tell you why we came to Minnesota. It was when I found out you had 15,000 blacks here. Black people don't go to ball games, but they'll fill up a rassling ring and put up such a chant it'll scare you to death. It's unbelievable. We came here because you've got good, hard-working, white people here."

A newspaper story about the remarks ran a few days later, the day of the team's final game. There was talk of players boycotting. They ended up playing, but star player Rod Carew, whom Griffith had also singled out for scorn at the Lions Club, soon left for California.

The NAACP called for a boycott of the team. After initially trying to deny he'd said those things, Griffith later apologized, claiming he wasn't racist, just inebriated, when he spoke. Griffith owned the team for more than twenty years. A statue of him stood outside the Twins' home ballpark, Target Field, from its opening in 2010 to June 2020.

black faces entertaining." The discrimination was "terrible, absolutely terrible," noted Dick Mayes, who played with saxophonist Percy Hughes. "You never saw black bands down there." But that doesn't mean there weren't any Black musicians. They had been performing for decades in other venues, including speakeasies, illegal nightclubs, strip clubs (as John Nelson did with his Prince Rogers Trio), and legal night clubs in north Minneapolis's own Black neighborhoods.

Music had long thrived along Olson Memorial Highway in the Near North neighborhood. Duke Ellington and Count Basie are among those who performed at several clubs that brought jazz to the Twin Cities; there were also several underground venues along the stretch during

Prohibition. The housing covenants and other discriminatory practices that kept so many nonwhite people from buying homes elsewhere in Minneapolis eventually brought Jews and Blacks together in north Minneapolis. As Swensson notes, this helped build the music scene:

> On the surface, thanks in large part to the majority Jewish population that had settled in the area and opened businesses along Plymouth and Olson Memorial, the Near North neighborhood appeared to passersby to be a predominantly white, buttoned-up place.
>
> But vibrating just underneath the surface was an exciting culture of cutting-edge music and black nightlife. As the next generation of young black musicians came of age in North Minneapolis, the allure of these underground spaces was downright intoxicating.

It wasn't just in the area of music that Blacks in Minneapolis felt invisible.

Bryant and Sixth Avenues North (soon to be Olson Memorial Highway), Near North Minneapolis, 1936. *Photo by A. F. Raymond, MNHS Collections*

Plymouth Avenue

There had been a time when north Minneapolis was a hub of Black business and economic activity—not available to African Americans elsewhere in the city. At one point in 1937 it was so chock-full of pedestrians that the Black-owned Minneapolis *Spokesman* newspaper compared the stretch to Beale Street in Memphis. "The most famous corner on Sixth Avenue North is the Lyndale Avenue corner where for years the colored people of that section have congregated."

Sixth Avenue North later became Olson Memorial Highway, named for Governor Floyd Olson, who was born on the north side and later died in office. When it was widened into a highway in the late 1930s, it cut Near North in half. Gone was the pedestrian ambiance and community feel.

After the war, housing discrimination against Jews eased, and Jewish families started moving to the suburbs, but many maintained their businesses in north Minneapolis. Some former neighbors resented this racial inequity. After a few incidents of looting in August 1966, Mayor Arthur Naftalin—a former aide to, and protégé of, Hubert Humphrey, and also the city's first Jewish mayor—met with leaders of the Black community and acknowledged the lack of opportunities. He reached out to his network for help, and across the city some jobs opened for Blacks. At the community's demand, a center called The Way, devoted to empowering young Black people, was established in an empty storefront on Plymouth Avenue.

But by the next summer, the promised progress had stalled. On July 19, an argument broke out during Minneapolis's Aquatennial Torchlight Parade, which led to accusations that a Black woman had been mistreated. As a crowd of African Americans walking up from the parade site converged on Plymouth Avenue, violence erupted. Someone set the Knox Food Market, a Jewish-owned business, on fire, and someone threw Molotov cocktails at the home of the local alderman.

Harry Davis, a well-respected leader in the Black community, and Josie Johnson, then an adviser to the mayor, encouraged Naftalin not to have the police sweep the street. The National Guard was called in to maintain order but also to be a calmer force than the city's own cops, many of whom wanted to take a harder line. After sporadic incidents the second night, a peaceful dance held at The Way helped calm the neighborhood enough to end the unrest. No one died, but several people were injured and several businesses, many Jewish owned, were vandalized or destroyed.

Minneapolis wasn't alone; 1967 became known as the "long, hot summer" because of 159 instances of unrest that occurred in cities across the country. Civil rights leader Rev. Martin Luther King Jr. had spoken to students at the University of Minnesota a few months prior. His words would seem prescient. "I see no more dangerous development than the build-up of central cities surrounded by white suburbs," he noted. King had chastised his largely white audience for not being genuinely committed to the hard work of racial equality. Simply speaking out against the most racist figures in the news wasn't enough. Legislative victories, he said,

> had rectified some evils of the South, but did little to improve conditions for millions of Negroes in teeming ghettoes of the North. . . . I have an obligation to vigorously condemn the conditions in our society that cause people to feel they have no other alternative than to engage in self-defeating violence.
>
> Riots are the language of the unheard. Our summers of riots are caused by our winters of delay.

Davis later led a coalition that joined business and community groups to work to address the injustices in the community. When Rev. King was assassinated in 1968, Davis and the still-new coalition worked to largely prevent the rioting that happened in other cities.

Another aftermath of the summer unrest was voter backlash. When Naftalin decided not to seek reelection in 1969, Charles Stenvig used a "law and order" campaign—similar to the one George Wallace used to run for president in 1968—to win the mayorship. Stenvig had been the bombastic head of the Minneapolis police union. He thought the police reaction should have been stronger on Plymouth Avenue, and he pledged to "take the handcuffs off the police." Harry Davis opposed Stenvig four years later as the city's first-ever Black mayoral candidate; Davis lost.

AIM

Almost exactly one year after the long, hot summer in north Minneapolis, a group of eighty-six people, mostly women and children, showed up at a meeting on Plymouth Avenue, about seven blocks east of The Way. This group was made up of Native Americans of many nations, meeting to discuss what had become the broken promises of the government's relocation program. Plenty of Indigenous people had moved to Minneapolis for the promised good jobs, but most had found only despair. The jobs they could find paid little, and their community faced widespread discrimination and violence, often inflicted by police.

"The men in our community were defeated by unemployment and alcohol," remembered Clyde Bellecourt, who helped organize this meeting. "The men didn't see a future." The women, meanwhile, "were raising the kids; they looked the future in the eye every day. It was always the women who stood up first for the Movement, even though many of them never received credit for their contributions." The group formed that day was the Concerned Indian American (CIA) Coalition; it wanted to improve these conditions for Natives, who were often ignored in the civil rights debates of the time that focused on Blacks and white people.

The group was soon renamed the American Indian Movement, known as AIM. Its first efforts included an AIM Patrol (a citizens' patrol in the Phillips neighborhood that monitored police interactions with Natives) and working to found the Indian Health Board (1969) and the Legal Rights Center (1970), which helped find attorneys to represent Native people.

In 1970 AIM members occupied the US Naval Air Station near Fort Snelling, arguing it was abandoned federal property and thus should revert to Indigenous ownership. The group wanted a building for a

Clyde Bellecourt

Clyde Bellecourt recounts how the name of the Minneapolis group that wanted to address problems in the Native American community was changed from Concerned Indian American (CIA) Coalition to American Indian Movement (AIM) in this excerpt from his autobiography, *The Thunder Before the Storm*:

> An older woman named Alberta Downwind came up with the idea.
>
> "Call yourself AIM," she said.
>
> "AIM?" I said. "What does that mean?"
>
> "American Indian Movement," she replied. "You're always aiming to do this or that. We should call the group AIM."
>
> "Well, I want to drop that word Indian," I argued. "We are finally through with that word. We're not from India."
>
> Alberta grabbed me by the arm and said, "Listen, *Indian* is the word that they used to oppress us. *Indian* is the word we'll use to gain our freedom."
>
> I said, "Right on."

school for Native children. At one point, Senator Walter Mondale arrived for a meeting with the group only to find they had been arrested, which drew his ire. Two people charged with crimes related to the takeover were freed when the trial ended with a hung jury.

After the Indian Education Act was passed in 1972, Indigenous peoples had far more influence over how their children were educated. AIM founded two community schools, Heart of the Earth Survival School in Minneapolis and Red School House in St. Paul. These survival schools were the antithesis of the boarding schools that had traumatized generations of Indigenous peoples: they taught Native students in ways that didn't erase their history or identity.

Dennis Banks, Clyde Bellecourt, and Russell Means are often listed as AIM's leaders, but women played crucial roles, including Pat Bellanger, who worked with the group for nearly fifty years and came to be known as Grandma AIM.

Heart of the Earth Survival School. *Photo by Dick Bancroft*

AIM organizations in other relocation cities joined together to sponsor marches on Washington to demand religious freedom and other legislation to support sovereignty. The group gained notoriety for its part in a seventy-one-day occupation at Wounded Knee in South Dakota that grew violent. This controversial action splintered the group. Its branches have participated in the international movement for Indigenous rights and remain active today.

Freedom to Marry and LGBTQIA+ Rights

In the final month of 1969, first-year University of Minnesota student Jack Baker called Michael McConnell with some news. Baker had been researching Minnesota's marriage law and discovered it didn't actually state that a union must be between a man and a woman. It was silent on gender. Therefore, Baker told McConnell, they could get married.

The pair had met and fallen in love three years earlier. McConnell wanted to marry and Baker promised to find a way. Baker had become the first president of Minnesota's first gay rights organization, Fight

Mayor for a Day

When former city council member Al Hofstede won the mayor's election in 1973, it put him in line to become Minneapolis's fortieth mayor. But another man beat him to it—for a day.

This quirk in city history happened on New Year's Eve 1973. Incumbent mayor Charles Stenvig had been defeated and Hofstede was about to take over. But a day before the official transition, Stenvig resigned.

Before becoming mayor (as a "law and order" independent candidate), Stenvig had been a police lieutenant and outspoken head of the police union. He quit the mayorship a day early to return to the police department as deputy chief. It's not clear why he did this, though such a move likely improved the pension he would soon draw. He also may have thought Hofstede might make him police chief (he didn't).

The move meant the president of the Minneapolis City Council—Dick Erdall—became mayor, if only for a few hours. Erdall made no official moves. It's not even clear he went to the mayor's office at city hall. But it counts. The city's website lists the dates of Erdall's tenure as fortieth mayor as December 31, 1973–December 31, 1973. Erdall also ranks as the most recent Republican mayor of Minneapolis.

Repression of Erotic Expression (FREE). It was founded in May 1969, a month before the Stonewall Uprising in New York City.

In May 1970, news reporters and cameras in tow, the two went to the Hennepin County Courthouse in downtown Minneapolis to apply for a marriage license—the first documented time a same-sex couple did so. They paid the ten-dollar fee but soon were denied a license. They took the case to court, and also went to court when McConnell lost his library job at the University of Minnesota following the publicity.

But while those court cases played out, the couple devised a new plan. Michael McConnell *adopted* Jack Baker, to gain family tax benefits and because it wasn't explicitly illegal to marry someone you had adopted. During the adoption process, Baker legally changed his name to Pat Lyn McConnell. Then they moved to Mankato to establish residency before

Jack Baker (right) and James Michael McConnell (left) apply for a marriage license in Minneapolis, May 1970. *MNHS Collections 015051-16*

McConnell went to the Blue Earth County Courthouse (alone) to apply for a marriage license for Pat and Michael.

The license was approved and the men were married September 3, 1971. They later lost their original court case, but that mattered less after the successful second attempt. They were married. After a flurry of attention and public speaking, the two withdrew from public life.

The work for LGBTQIA+ rights continued, however. Even in the early 1970s, Minneapolis was known for its strong gay community—a community that could offer support when the broader public wouldn't. This support was important when the HIV/AIDS crisis broke into the national consciousness in the early 1980s. Gay men and lesbians were just as likely to be targets in Minneapolis as anywhere, losing jobs and leases, not to mention friends and family. One of the nation's first gay community centers was the Gay House in Minneapolis. As the HIV/AIDS crisis widened, groups like the Minnesota AIDS Project and the Aliveness Project worked with people with the disease.

In 1993, Minnesota became the eighth state to ban discrimination based on sexual orientation and the first to do so for transgender people. Discrimination was banned in areas including housing, employment, public accommodations, and access to credit. With support from a campaign called "It's Time, Minnesota," two legislators from Minneapolis— Senator Allan Spear, a gay man, and Representative Karen Clark, a lesbian—marshaled the legislation to passage. After having heard for years the argument against such protections (i.e., that homosexuality was a choice), Spear told his colleagues before the vote, "Let me tell you, I'm a fifty-five-year-old gay man and I'm not just going through a phase!" The law also included language stating that the state doesn't condone "homosexuality or bisexuality or any equivalent lifestyle."

A few years after the measure passed, Congress defined marriage in the 1996 Defense of Marriage Act as a union of a man and a woman. The next year, Minnesota followed with its own state version. The 1993 law had banned many kinds of discrimination based on sexual orientation; the 1997 law defined marriage as a union of a man and a woman.

Gradually, then swiftly, social acceptance and support for marriage equality grew. In 2012, after several states had passed voter referenda to ban same-sex marriage, Minnesota became the first state to *reject* such a referendum. The following year, lawmakers legalized same-sex marriage in Minnesota. Just after midnight on the day the law took effect, hundreds of people at Minneapolis City Hall witnessed Margaret Miles and Cathy ten Broeke get married—the first of forty-two weddings Mayor R. T. Rybak performed in the wee hours on the marble steps.

The US Supreme Court did the same nationally in 2015. In 2017, more history: two transgender candidates, Andrea Jenkins and Phillipe Cunningham, won seats on the Minneapolis City Council—a first for any major US city.

When same-sex marriage was legalized, Jack Baker and Michael McConnell did not apply for a new license or get married again. To do so would suggest their 1971 license wasn't legal. Its legitimacy was affirmed in 2018 when a court ruled the marriage valid, even though Blue Earth County hadn't officially recorded the license when officials learned the applicants were men. The ruling (along with a subsequent decision affirming their eligibility for Social Security spousal benefits) confirmed what Baker and McConnell had believed and known all along: theirs was the first legal, same-sex marriage in the United States.

Speaking to a reporter in 2019, McConnell added, "the bullies with power have been bullying us for all this time, and we won."

Social movements in Minneapolis in the 1960s and 1970s took place in a city and state that prided themselves on progressive reform and economic success. Minnesota won national acclaim for 1971 legislation that dramatically raised income and sales taxes to allow the state to pay more of the costs of school spending—and enabled local governments to decrease property taxes. Dubbed the "Minnesota Miracle," it landed the state's governor Wendell Anderson and an unfortunate northern pike on the cover of *Time* magazine in 1973. Unlike previous national coverage that highlighted Minneapolis's antisemitism or government corruption, this piece proclaimed Minnesota a "state that works." As the state's largest city, Minneapolis asserted a strong claim to that identity.

The state had enjoyed above-average economic growth in the postwar years. Its fledgling computer companies boomed, with Engineering Research Associates (later part of UNIVAC, then Sperry Rand), Control Data Corporation, Honeywell, Unisys, IBM-Rochester, and others helping to create the nation's computer industry. Medical devices, food companies, banking, and many other industries provided a healthy, diversified regional economy. The city's dominance over a vast hinterland was echoed in the territory covered by the Minneapolis Federal Reserve Bank, established in 1914 to serve Minnesota, Montana, North and South Dakota, northwestern Wisconsin, and the Upper Peninsula of Michigan.

The Twin Cities came to be home to a relatively extraordinary number of Fortune 500 companies. A survey from the Ford Foundation in the 1970s had found the Cities were second only to New York in support for the arts. As the cover of *Time* had proclaimed, "the good life in Minnesota" seemed like the real deal.

The Good Life In Minnesota

Gov. Wendell Anderson

Governor Wendell Anderson representing the good life in Minnesota for *Time* magazine, August 13, 1973

Popular culture popped as well. *The Mary Tyler Moore Show,* a sitcom broadcast from 1970 to 1977, showed a single, happy woman having a successful career in Minneapolis. And late in the decade, a style of music taking shape would soon become internationally heralded as the Minneapolis Sound, led by a genius from north Minneapolis named Prince, who performed every instrument on every song on his debut studio album in 1978, *For You.*

By the 1980s, Minnesota's professional sports teams had gained loyal followings and produced memorable teams, but no championships.

Football. The Vikings, with quarterback Fran Tarkenton and a defensive line known as the Purple People Eaters, went to four Super Bowl games during the 1970s (including three in four years) but lost them all.

Baseball. The Minnesota Twins started their time in Minnesota strong, advancing to a World Series and two playoff series (all of which were lost) by 1970 before settling into a decade-plus of mediocre play. They bounced back to win the World Series in 1987 and 1991.

Ice hockey. The Minnesota North Stars never captured their sport's championship, the Stanley Cup, during their time in Minnesota. But that didn't make their fans any less invested. Minnesota now has the Minnesota Wild, who continue the search for a Cup.

Basketball. Professional basketball didn't return to Minneapolis until the late 1980s. The Timberwolves also are without a title to date, but the women's pro team, the Lynx, won four titles during the 2010s.

Soccer. After decades of attempts to establish professional soccer in the United States, with teams including the Minnesota Kicks and Minnesota Strikers, Minnesota United became a Major League Soccer franchise in 2017.

However, studies and data that proclaimed Minneapolis's above-averageness weren't the whole story. As the city grew more racially and ethnically diverse, its disparities and inequities also grew.

Prince

In 1958, seven years after Mount Sinai Hospital opened so that Jewish doctors could admit their patients, a young Black woman named Mattie Shaw was admitted, ready to give birth. She lived nearby—on a street that would front I-35W when it came through the neighborhood years later—with her husband, John Nelson.

The two were musicians and had met at the Phyllis Wheatley House on the north side, where John's group often performed. On June 7, Shaw gave birth to a son, Prince Rogers Nelson. John later told a television interviewer he gave his son the name Prince "because I wanted him to do everything I really intended to do."

The family moved to north Minneapolis when Prince was still a baby. As he navigated challenges, including epileptic seizures as a boy, young Prince (called Skipper as a kid) would follow his parents toward music. With downtown venues off-limits to Black musicians, Prince's father found other options, like performing at strip clubs. He later recalled times when someone would tell him during a gig that his son had snuck in and was watching, though Nelson added he could never find Prince when he went looking.

Along with friends André Cymone (born André Anderson), Morris Day, James "Jimmy Jam" Harris, and Terry Lewis, Prince was exposed to Minneapolis's R & B and soul music scenes, as well as the mainstream classic rock their white classmates listened to, in the southside schools they were bused to as part of an integration program. "I went to school with the rich kids who didn't like having me there," Prince told his biographer, Dan Piepenbring. And Piepenbring later wrote in the *New Yorker*, "In retrospect, he believed that Minnesota at that time was no more enlightened than segregationist Alabama had been."

Prince and his friends found refuge at north Minneapolis hangouts like The Way, which had a house band called The Family. Prince sometimes played during jam sessions; he soon formed a band called Grand Central.

In channeling music from both white and Black worlds, Prince soon created the unique Minneapolis Sound—which, among other traits, replaced

Prince performing at the Orpheum Theatre, February 9, 1980, with Dez Dickerson at right. *Photo by Greg Helgeson*

horns with synthesizers and drums with drum machines. The Sound, as detailed by Andrea Swensson in her book *Got to Be Something Here*, was the culmination of "two generations of political upheaval, rebellion, and artistic passion" in the Twin Cities—all of which influenced Prince.

Twin Cities radio stations had a long history of not playing music created by the local Black community. "It was a very vanilla market," Steven Greenberg told Swensson. Greenberg's band, Lipps Inc., produced one of the biggest hits to ever come out of Minneapolis—the song "Funkytown." "Even though 'Funkytown' was recorded by a hometown artist, the local radio market was the last to pick it up," Swensson added.

Bobby Z noted the same thing happened with Prince's band, in which he played drums. The music took off in the South first, and although he "had made his debut playing under his own name at the Capri Theater in 1979, [Prince] was still an unknown quantity to the majority of music fans living in the Twin Cities," writes Swensson. Swensson also notes that the discrimination by Twin Cities radio stations might have helped Prince. Because he was also influenced by the rock and roll and other white music he heard on the radio, Swensson argues that might explain in part how he was able to create music that appealed across racial lines.

In time, Prince started winning Grammys, an Oscar, and innumerable other awards. Any attempt to list his best work only risks leaving stuff out, though 1984 is a key year because the album and movie versions of the now iconic *Purple Rain* were released.

Prince was an international superstar and put Minneapolis on the map. First Avenue, the bus-station-turned-music-venue, featured prominently in the movie *Purple Rain* and became a tourist attraction, as did Paisley Park, the building where Prince lived and worked in the suburb of Chanhassen.

His brand also became a mystery, as he shunned most media interviews. He also guarded his work fiercely, not because it was mysterious but because it was part of his lifelong activism. It took years before he gained control of his master recordings, long after he had changed his name to a symbol during the 1990s in an attempt to break a contract with Warner Bros.

As Piepenbring recalled from a conversation, Prince felt "black communities would restore wealth by safeguarding their musicians' master recordings and all their intellectual property, and they would protect that wealth, hiring their own police, founding their own schools, and making covenants on their own terms."

Prince later supported the Black Lives Matter movement that grew from the police shootings in the national consciousness. He sent money to the family of Trayvon Martin, the unarmed teen shot to death by a neighborhood-watch volunteer in Florida in 2012. He also anonymously supported several organizations and nonprofits in north Minneapolis and held fundraisers throughout his career for local organizations.

Throughout his stardom, he never left. "I stayed in Minneapolis because Minneapolis made me," he told biographer Piepenbring. "You have to give back."

Years of performing left Prince in significant pain. In his fifties, he became addicted to painkillers, like so many Americans during the opioid crisis that exploded in the 2010s. He overdosed, accidentally, in his home on April 21, 2016.

The world grieved and looked to Minneapolis. And the city shone. People flocked to Paisley Park to mourn. A quickly arranged concert outside First Avenue drew thousands. The show featured local artists who had been influenced by and even worked with Prince, including Lizzo, who was just breaking through to national stardom.

Prince was the biggest megastar to come out of Minneapolis. His music crossed racial barriers in a city whose radio stations initially didn't play him (and countless others) because he was Black. That night, none of that mattered. Singing along to Prince songs in a crowd of thousands was a beautiful moment of togetherness.

CHAPTER 11

Refugee, Rebirth, and Reconciliation

On October 1, 2005, a flight from New York arrived at Minneapolis–St. Paul International Airport. Its passengers included an extended family of eight heading to their new home. They had secured the right to emigrate to the United States after escaping a brutal civil war that had raged for more than a decade in their home country in Africa, Somalia. They had most recently been living in neighboring Kenya. Mukhtar Ibrahim, then seventeen, vividly remembers the reunion at the airport with his brother, Mustafa, who already lived in the Cities. "Seeing someone you hadn't for a decade, it was a very joyous moment," Ibrahim recalled.

Mukhtar and his family joined the largest-ever Somali diaspora, numbering an estimated seventy-four thousand in 2019. While that number represents less than 1.5 percent of Minnesota's entire population, it's too large for some people.

Almost exactly eleven years after the Ibrahims' jubilant reunion inside one of the nation's busiest airports, a starkly different scene played out at the same airport. In the waning days of the presidential campaign, Republican nominee Donald Trump spoke to more than five thousand mostly white supporters inside an airplane hangar. A few thousand more stood outside. He would soon surprise politicos by almost winning the state. In Minnesota, a state that hadn't voted for a Republican for president in forty-four years—the longest such streak in the country—he fell just 1.5 percent short of the vote required to win. During his forty-minute speech, he singled out Somali refugees as a "disaster taking place in

Minnesota." Mukhtar Ibrahim, now in his late twenties, had become a Somali American journalist. He wasn't at that rally, but he did cover President Trump three years later, when he returned for a rally in downtown Minneapolis. Trump continued demagoguing Somalis, including the Somali who now represented Minneapolis in Congress ("a disgrace to our country," he called Representative Ilhan Omar). The crowd booed at the mention of Somalis.

"I didn't know we were hated like that," one American man of Somali descent later told a reporter. "Donald Trump is one man, but what scares me is the amount of support he has." Ibrahim also included Somali voices in his story, which mentioned their resolve to work to prevent Trump's reelection in 2020. Ibrahim posted the story on Sahan Journal, the news website he founded that covers immigrants and refugees. The next day, someone left a voicemail calling Ibrahim a racial slur (twice) and telling him to "go back to where you came from." He had received hate mail before, but this was the first time he forwarded anything to the FBI. "I think it's someone who doesn't like my presence here and someone who could potentially now carry out the violence if he has the means," Ibrahim told the *New York Times*.

This vitriol was not at all universal; most city and community leaders, including the mayor, repeatedly noted how much they appreciated and welcomed Somalis and other immigrants. One thing they didn't directly say, but which is true, is that Minneapolis had immigrants to thank for reversing a discouraging, decades-long trend of population decline.

Vietnam

As US troops left Southeast Asia in the 1970s, governments the Americans had propped up fell in Cambodia, Laos, and South Vietnam. The US departure created millions of refugees. Those fleeing South Vietnam, who had fought alongside American soldiers, were expected. But thousands also escaped Cambodia and Laos, including Hmong fighters; they had helped the CIA wage a secret war in those countries that was only disclosed to the American public in 1971, with the release of the Pentagon

Papers. Because the United States had essentially caused the crisis, Congress voted in 1975 to allow these refugees to enter the country.

Lutheran and Catholic social service agencies led the efforts in the Twin Cities, helping resettle refugees. The state later opened its own resettlement office, and Congress passed a refugee law in 1980 that further increased the rate of arrivals. The process wasn't perfect; private organizations and later government organizations struggled to find resources, especially as the number of refugees grew. Critics also issued the familiar charge that the refugees would steal jobs from Americans. Instead, many of them opened their own small businesses in parts of cities thought to be dead or dying.

A structure to manage resettlement eventually took shape. By 2019, an estimated eighty-eight thousand Hmong and thirty thousand Vietnamese lived in Minnesota, a majority of whom were born in the United States. Most also lived in the Twin Cities, which has the largest Hmong population of any US metropolitan area.

Numbers Increase

As the country's suburban population grew, several big cities in the Midwest and Rust Belt saw the same kind of population and economic declines Minneapolis (and St. Paul) experienced. The largest population decline in Minneapolis was during the 1970s—a stunning 14 percent. By 1980, the city was its smallest since the 1910s and still nearly 90 percent white. Reagan-era federal funding cuts would soon exacerbate economic declines.

But the 1980s also saw the arrival of the first major wave of new immigrants to Minneapolis since the early part of the century. This influx helped keep the population dip during the 1980s to less than one percent before a population increase during the 1990s—the first in a half century. That 1990s increase was partially from the arrival of refugees escaping war in Somalia, utilizing the same network of Lutheran and Catholic social service agencies created during the arrival of Southeast Asian refugees.

But there was also a *quadrupling* of Minneapolis's Hispanic population. By 2000, eight percent of the city's population was Hispanic or Latino, up from two percent in 1990. Many of these arrivals settled around Nicollet Avenue and Lake Street in the Whittier and Lyndale neighborhoods of south Minneapolis.

In addition, the Twin Cities became a leading destination for Black people seeking a better life after the rust-belt economy further tanked in the early 1980s. They arrived from the Chicago, Gary (Indiana), and Milwaukee areas, nearly tripling the state's Black population between 1980 (fifty thousand) and the late 1990s (140,000).

Today, Minneapolis is still below its 1950s population peak, but the 2020 census showed a 12 percent jump during the 2010s—the largest increase since the 1930s—that once again put the city above 400,000 residents.

Immigrant Hubs

Since the 1980s, the arrival of new immigrants, refugees, and migrants has brought economic rejuvenation to certain neighborhoods, while also continuing to relegate marginalized people to specific and historically redlined quarters.

One example is Cedar-Riverside, also called the West Bank. This neighborhood between downtown and the University of Minnesota has a long immigrant history. Early on, it was dubbed "Snoose Boulevard," an enclave for Scandinavian immigrants; later racial mixing made it a target for redlining. Twenty thousand people lived on the West Bank in 1910—double today's population. It remains one of the city's most densely populated neighborhoods.

Immigrants from Eastern Europe arrived after World War II before the neighborhood became a counterculture center during the 1960s—a "Haight-Ashbury of the Midwest." The area was considered "blighted" by the city's white leaders during that decade of urban renewal. As a result, properties were bought and buildings razed to make room for the city's largest-ever housing development project, Cedar Square West (now Riverside Plaza). The tactics of developers, who destroyed historic

A Trailblazing Cedar-Riverside Activist in City Hall

Brian Coyle became prominent in Cedar-Riverside during the 1970s for his activism in favor of tenants' rights and against both the Vietnam War and public subsidies for stadiums. He lost the stadium battle in 1982, when the Metrodome opened after years of deliberations.

Coyle was elected to the city council in 1983, making him Minneapolis's first openly gay city council member. He was council vice president in 1991, when the body passed Minnesota's first municipal domestic-partner ordinance that made city employees in same-sex relationships eligible for sick and bereavement leave.

In April 1991, Coyle became one of the nation's first elected officials to announce he was HIV positive. He died four months later. In 1993, the city opened a new community center named for Coyle in Cedar-Riverside, about two thousand feet east of the Metrodome he long opposed.

Brian Coyle, about 1985. *MNHS*

buildings and chose not to consult residents, brought protests and a scaling back of the original plan to build a "New Town in Town."

The plaza, which opened in 1973 and is home to nearly five thousand people, includes several apartment towers that have a distinctive place on the Minneapolis skyline. Southeast Asian refugees arrived in the 1970s and 1980s, followed by Hispanics and East Africans in the 1990s. Somali-owned businesses opened throughout Cedar-Riverside, along with Dar Al-Hijrah, the first mosque in Minnesota, in 1998.

Contemporary refugee populations include many who came through secondary migration. After initially settling elsewhere in the United States, they moved to Minnesota to join family or find work.

Efforts especially by social service agencies gave the Twin Cities a reputation as a friendly place for refugees and immigrants. And why not? This is the state whose population was *40 percent* foreign-born in 1890, compared to *11 percent* nationally. By 2016, the Pew Research Center noted that Minnesota had more refugees per capita than any state.

But as with all generalizations, there are contradictions. Some challenges are similar for all new arrivals, no matter their timing or nationality. Scandinavians in the late 1800s had the same difficulties learning English as Somalis later would. However, Somalis have also faced racial and religious discrimination for being dark-skinned Muslims. After the terrorist attacks of September 11, 2001, the Twin Cities Somali community denounced Islamic terrorism and called Islam a religion of peace—something President George W. Bush echoed during a visit to a Washington, DC, mosque after the attacks.

Still, Somali Americans faced new discrimination from hate groups, and the FBI put community members under surveillance. When money-transfer businesses, called hawalas, were closed for fear they could be used to funnel cash to terrorist organizations, Somali Minnesotans found it harder to send funds to relatives in Somalia or at refugee camps in Kenya. This was a major problem: the United Nations estimated that Somalia received $1 billion in global remittances as it struggled to emerge from a generation of war.

Later in the first decade of the twenty-first century, terrorist groups started recruiting on social media and convinced a handful of young Minneapolis men of East African descent to fight in Somalia and Syria. Most who did so died, and the Minneapolis community struggled with the loss, even as the FBI ramped up investigations. This radicalization included just a few people among tens of thousands of Somalis, but it became fodder for demagogues seeking to paint them as "a disaster."

President Donald Trump's executive order in 2017 banned new immigration from Somalia and several other majority-Muslim nations. Just forty-eight people came to Minnesota from Somalia in 2018, down from more than fourteen hundred in 2016.

Rebuilding

As new immigrants helped stem population decline and made Minneapolis home, city leaders continued to try to bolster downtown against competition from growing suburbs—and to rebuild other collapses in the city's fabric. During the 1960s, Nicollet Mall and the skyways were considered initial victories in that effort. During the 1970s and '80s, new buildings went up, from City Center to the Metrodome.

Other buildings came down, including an entire block of what had become seedy, rundown structures on Hennepin Avenue like Moby Dick's Bar, which promised a "whale of a drink" but became a whale of a problem for officials. Once leveled, Block E was an empty parking lot for more than a decade.

Other buildings were rehabbed, like Butler Square and the Orpheum Theatre, which singer Bob Dylan owned for most of the 1980s. And at least one building was moved. Over two weeks in 1999, the Shubert Theater was raised and methodically moved on rubber tires about two blocks down Hennepin Avenue, where it became the Hennepin Center for the Arts.

The city also found a new area for redevelopment. The riverfront, covered with vast rail yards and abandoned flour mills, had been called "the backside of the city"—in a report prepared *by the city!* The Washburn A Mill, a cornerstone of the city's milling history, sat abandoned

Stadiums

After the dynastic Minneapolis Lakers won five basketball championships in twelve years and left Minneapolis for Los Angeles in 1960, the
city was without a professional sports team for two decades. The teams
instead were located in the suburb of Bloomington to avoid aggravating
a Minneapolis vs. St. Paul rivalry. But Metropolitan Stadium had actually
been financed with bonds backed by the city of Minneapolis—St. Paul
didn't help fund it. In looking for a replacement, Minneapolis leaders
now wanted any stadium they helped build to be in the city.

When it opened, the multi-use Metrodome housed baseball's Minnesota Twins and football's Minnesota Vikings and University of Minnesota
Gophers. After hosting a Super Bowl, an NCAA Final Four, and two World
Series—and after a couple of dramatic, inflatable-roof collapses during
snowstorms—the Metrodome came down in 2014, and U.S. Bank Stadium was built in its place. TCF Bank Stadium opened on the university
campus in 2009 to house the Gophers, and Target Field opened across
downtown in 2010 to house the Twins.

Hubert H. Humphrey Metrodome, 2007. *Photo by Bobak Ha'Eri, CC by 3.0*

for years and was nearly destroyed by fire in 1991. Across the river, the final mill operating on the falls, Pillsbury A, shut down in 2003.

Pillsbury A became lofts for artists. Washburn A became the Mill City Museum, built within the retrofitted ruins of the mill. The Guthrie Theater built a new facility near the falls, and developers refurbished a stretch on the east bank called St. Anthony Main. The Stone Arch Bridge, its days carrying trains long over, became a pedestrian bridge.

The redevelopment boom arguably began with an immigrant in 1968, when Reiko Weston built a new restaurant within the shell of a burned-down mill. Fuji-Ya had floor-to-ceiling windows on the building's east side, which pointed patrons to once again look at the river—just as all the development to come would do.

After Fuji-Ya closed in 1990, the site again remained abandoned for decades until Owamni opened in 2021. The restaurant—instantly nationally acclaimed—focused on Indigenous cuisine, using only ingredients that would have been available to those who lived on the land before colonization. The business brought the area's history full circle: its name is derived from the Dakota word for the nearby falls that are sacred to Native peoples and that are the reason there is a Minneapolis.

Gaps

This redevelopment—all made in the name of trying to keep downtown vibrant—had limits. For all the economic growth and celebration of Minneapolis's idyllic image, disparities between white people and communities of color continued to grow. The desperation that led to violence on Plymouth Avenue and the founding of groups like AIM continued.

In 1995, gang wars and drive-by shootings resulted in a record ninety-seven murders in Minneapolis. The per capita murder rate that year was higher than New York City's. The city became known as "Murderapolis," thanks in part to a popular T-shirt at the time. Mayor Sharon Sayles Belton—the city's first female and first Black mayor—oversaw implementation of a controversial computer system (similar to what New York had) that used data to determine where to deploy police. That drew criticism of racial profiling, but there was also a drop in serious crime.

The disparities have persisted. The No Child Left Behind Act of 2001 mandated more public reporting of student achievement. Data was no longer broken down by school or grade—where blemishes could be glossed over—but by race. This forced white Minneapolis—and white America—to face what communities of color had been saying all along: the disparities are real. The disparities in Minneapolis and Minnesota soon ranked among the highest in the nation.

The early 2000s also brought years of state cuts of direct aid to cities, called Local Government Aid—a nearly 25 percent drop between 2002 and 2013 (adjusted for inflation). This happened as the federal government was asking cities after the 2001 terrorist attacks to bolster emergency response and terrorism planning. The decade ended with a housing market collapse that caused the Great Recession, the most severe economic crisis since the Great Depression.

The housing collapse hit African American families harder because wealth among Blacks had been more connected to home ownership than other types of wealth. Unscrupulous lenders also had steered Black borrowers to subprime mortgages, which featured high down payments and interest rates that are offered to borrowers who wouldn't qualify for conventional mortgages. Many, of course, live in redlined neighborhoods. African American residents were more likely to lose their homes.

There were also more evictions. One study found that between 2013 and 2015, nearly half of all renter households in north Minneapolis's two zip codes had an eviction filing. But only three percent of such households saw eviction filings in the affluent, mostly white southwest neighborhood of Linden Hills. The city's own Public Housing Authority—the largest landlord in the county—was found to be the entity that sought the most evictions.

Sociologist Matthew Desmond explored this issue in his Pulitzer Prize–winning book *Evicted*, noting that low-income women are more likely to be evicted than low-income men. In short, he argues that because of generations of mass incarceration, Black men have been locked up. But because of evictions, Black women have been locked out.

In the midst of these difficulties, a tornado cut through the north side in May 2011, killing two, damaging or destroying thirty-seven hundred structures (mostly homes), causing about $80 million in damage, and displacing many. The city later learned that those who needed help were mostly already on some kind of public assistance, and those with jobs were spending, on average, 70 percent of their income on housing. People already struggling with finances now faced unaffordable challenges—some as simple as buying a tarp to cover a hole in a roof.

A response team soon emerged, funded with private donations and led by people from several northside organizations. "Much of north Minneapolis has been rebuilt," Mayor R. T. Rybak noted in his memoir, *Pothole Confidential*. "But it will take much longer to fully understand the damage that can't be seen."

Most disparities that were baked into the fabric of the city sat quietly for generations, until they were thrust onto a global stage with the events of May 25, 2020.

CHAPTER 12

Saying Their Names

Darnella Frazier had walked countless times to Cup Foods, the small store near where she lived. On the evening of May 25, 2020, when she and her cousin went there for snacks, they happened upon police arresting a man outside the store. Something seemed wrong to Frazier. She sent her cousin inside and started recording the arrest on her phone.

A policeman was kneeling on the man's neck. "It wasn't right," she would later tell a courtroom. "He was suffering; he was in pain."

The man was forty-six-year-old George Floyd. Police had been called on a report that Floyd had used counterfeit money. After they pulled him from his car, Floyd resisted being put into a squad car, citing claustrophobia, and the officers laid him on the ground. They then pinned him, handcuffed, with officer Derek Chauvin kneeling on his neck.

Floyd pleaded that he couldn't breathe. Minutes passed. An ambulance arrived. Floyd was pronounced dead at a hospital.

The department's first public account of the encounter—titled "Man Dies After Medical Incident During Police Interaction"—made no mention of the kneeling that lasted more than nine minutes. But Frazier's video, which went viral online, showed what police had omitted.

The outrage was palpable and quick.

Something was different.

Maybe it was because it wasn't the first time. Floyd's death was at least the eleventh at the hands of Minneapolis police in the previous ten years.

Four years earlier, according to some witnesses, police shot a Black man named Jamar Clark while he was unarmed and handcuffed. He was reaching for an officer's gun and his DNA was on the gun, countered the police and prosecutors.

Eight months after that, a Black man named Philando Castile was pulled over in Falcon Heights, a St. Paul suburb. His girlfriend and her four-year-old daughter were also in the car. While retrieving his license, Castile told the officer he had a gun. The officer told him not to reach for it. Castile said he wasn't. A split second later, the officer had fired seven shots. Castile's girlfriend then used her phone to broadcast the immediate aftermath to the world through Facebook Live. The video appeared to show Castile drawing his last breath.

With both cases, demonstrations across the Twin Cities included highway shutdowns. After Clark's death, protestors occupied the street in front of a police station for eighteen days.

They were just two of several high-profile killings of Black and brown people by police brought into the public consciousness during the 2010s—in many cases, through the instant ability to photograph and record incidents with smartphones. Just as white Americans could no longer ignore issues like gaps in educational opportunities and achievement, so could they no longer ignore an issue that communities of color had protested for decades: police violence. But even after several years of protest, something was different after George Floyd died.

Maybe it's because the country was a few months into a global pandemic. People were largely working from home and not gathering socially because there was not yet a vaccine for COVID-19. The science, however, found COVID was less contagious outdoors. It was early summer. People headed outside.

Or maybe it's because George Floyd called out to his mother. At one point, amidst pleading that he couldn't breathe, Floyd cried, "Mom, I love you. I love you. Tell my kids I love them. I'm dead."

Floyd's mother, Larcenia, had died two years earlier.

In an instant, Minneapolis was the center of the world. Just as the "Shame of Minneapolis" magazine article brought national attention to the city in the early twentieth century, George Floyd brought an even wider reckoning in the twenty-first. Protests erupted across the country and the world, from Paris and London to Sydney and Hong Kong.

In Minneapolis, mourners gathered and occupied the intersection—38th and Chicago—where Floyd was killed. For many months afterward, community members and supporters maintained what became George Floyd Square as a healing space, creating memorials and holding gatherings while keeping the intersection closed to car traffic.

More protests rose up across the Twin Cities after Floyd's murder. During one march that shut down the I-35W bridge over the Mississippi River, a semitruck driver barreled through a crowd of protestors before stopping. Somehow, no one was injured.

Protests especially focused around the Third Precinct police headquarters, where the four police officers who responded to the call had worked until being fired the following day. Three days after Floyd's

Within days of George Floyd's murder, artists Xena Goldman, Cadex Herrera, and Greta McLain painted this mural at George Floyd Square. Maria Javier, Niko Alexander, Pablo Helm Hernandez, Rachel Breen, and bystanders also participated. *Photo by Laurie Shaull, May 31, 2020, CC by 2.0*

death, police abandoned the police station and the entire building soon was ablaze, its image broadcast across the globe.

In the ten days following Floyd's death, scores of businesses across the Twin Cities were damaged or destroyed by arson, or looting, or both. An Indian restaurant. A Black-owned distillery. A Target store. Cub Foods. Bank branches. A Walgreens. A post office. Lake Street—which had a long place in the city's history as a stretch where new immigrants got their start, in part because they had been shunned from other parts of the city—looked like a war zone. Curfews were in place across the region for several days.

In some cases, it would later be learned, agitators who weren't sympathetic to the cause of racial justice caused the worst vandalism and damage.

The chaos was amplified by a lack of city and police leadership. Reports would later detail how Mayor Jacob Frey disregarded the city's own emergency protocols, which led to delays in securing help from the Minnesota National Guard. Initial requests for the Guard, the report says, didn't include details on what Guard personnel were to do. Officers, meanwhile, failed to follow "consistent rules of engagement," which led to disparate treatment of protestors in matters like the use of tear gas and rubber bullets, some of which permanently injured people.

Two Sundays after Floyd's death, nine members of the Minneapolis City Council—a veto-proof majority—attended a rally in Powderhorn Park where the words "defund police" lined the stage. They pledged to dismantle the police department and create a new public safety system. The previous evening, Frey had been booed back into his home after telling a large crowd the opposite, that he did not support defunding police.

Defunding has different interpretations, but it usually means shifting resources to rely less on police to respond to emergencies. But "defund" also became a political divide, especially as Republicans used the rhetoric across the country during the 2020 election to turn voters away from Democrats who govern most big cities.

While Minneapolis did shift some funding from the police department, a total dismantling never happened, in part because the council

Black Lives Matter protest, London, June 6, 2020. *Photo by James Eades on Unsplash*

couldn't act without voter approval. A referendum in 2021 asked Minneapolis voters to create a new Department of Public Safety. It would also eliminate a requirement that the police force be a certain size, something the city's influential police union had advocated for in the 1960s. If passed, a police force would still exist, but the entire department would gain flexibility in how to keep the peace. Amendment opponents, however, used the defund rhetoric to rally the "no" vote. In addition, several hundred Minneapolis officers left the force after Floyd's death, filing disability and other claims, which left the department understaffed during an uptick in crime. The amendment failed, and six of the nine council members who stood on that stage either lost reelection or didn't run.

All four police officers in the Floyd case were indicted on state and federal charges. Derek Chauvin, who kneeled on Floyd's neck, went to trial in March 2021. During a month of testimony, prosecutors detailed how Chauvin failed to comply with department policy, while his defense pointed to Floyd's health history, including an enlarged heart, as the reason Floyd died.

Near the end of the trial, prosecutor Jerry Blackwell summed it this way: "You are told . . . that Mr. Floyd died because his heart was too big. . . . The truth of the matter is that the reason George Floyd is dead is because Mr. Chauvin's heart was too small."

The jury found Chauvin guilty in the murder of George Floyd, the first time a white police officer in Minnesota had ever been convicted of murdering a Black man.

Eight months later, Kim Potter became the second. She was convicted of killing Daunte Wright during a traffic stop in the Minneapolis suburb of Brooklyn Center on April 11, 2021, just nine days before Chauvin was convicted. Potter claimed she was reaching for her taser but instead fired her gun at Wright.

No officers were charged in Jamar Clark's death in 2015. In 2016 officer Jeronimo Yanez was charged in the death of Philando Castile but found not guilty of second-degree manslaughter and two counts of dangerous discharge of a firearm. But in the shootings of Floyd, Wright, and a third person in 2017, Justine Damond, officers were all convicted.

On February 2, 2022, Minneapolis police serving a warrant shot and killed Amir Locke. Locke was on a couch and under a blanket when police entered the apartment. He was also holding a gun and was shot about nine seconds after police arrived. His name was not on the search warrant.

While no charges were filed against the officer who shot Locke, the killing raised questions about no-knock warrants, whereby police break down a door and enter. While declining to press charges, Attorney General Keith Ellison and County Attorney Mike Freeman noted, "this tragedy may not have occurred absent the no-knock warrant used in this case."

When Mayor Frey campaigned for reelection in 2021, he said that no-knocks had ended. Such phrasing was also in campaign literature that advocated for Frey's reelection and against the referendum to revamp the police department structure. After Locke's death, Frey admitted his language during the campaign had become "more casual" and didn't reflect "the necessary precision or nuance."

Two months later, in April 2022, the Minnesota Department of Human Rights issued a scathing report after a two-year investigation into the Minneapolis Police Department. Findings outlined patterns of racial discrimination that broke the state's Human Rights Act and included what Black and brown people had long known: they were targeted for stops, searches, arrests, and use of force disproportionately more than white people. For example, Black people, about 19 percent of the city's population, were on the receiving end of 63 percent of all use-of-force incidents by Minneapolis police between 2010 and 2021.

"City and MPD leaders have been aware of the long-standing, disproportionate impact of race-based policing on people of color and Indigenous individuals, especially Black individuals," the report read. "Yet, these leaders have not collectively acted with the urgency, coordination, and intentionality necessary to address racial disparities to improve public safety."

Journalist Justin Ellis wouldn't have been surprised by that conclusion. The Minneapolis native wrote about growing up Black near Lake

Street in an article in the *Atlantic* after George Floyd's death. "When you're born into redlining," he wrote, "it has a way of making you believe that neighborhoods are the natural outcome of residents having a job and paying bills on time, not racism built through governments and banks and developers acting hand in hand."

Ellis also detailed a social science concept called "the Minnesota paradox" that Samuel Myers Jr. of the University of Minnesota has long studied: Minnesota is a state of plenty for white residents, but one of the worst places for members of minority groups. "The overwhelming sentiment among residents of Minnesota," Myers wrote in *Race Neutrality*, a 2018 book he coauthored, "is one of alarm and concern about these racial disparities but reluctance to attribute these disparities to systemic discrimination or racism."

The murder of George Floyd will be playing out in Minneapolis for as long as it takes the city to address that paradox.

What Next?

In June 2021, Darnella Frazier won a Pulitzer Prize. The prestigious journalism award went to the teenager who filmed George Floyd's murder for "highlighting the crucial role of citizens in journalists' quest for truth and justice."

It was one of many accolades for Frazier. But a few weeks earlier, in a statement posted to her Facebook and Instagram pages on the first anniversary of Floyd's death, she had rejected any idea that she was a hero. "Behind this smile, behind these awards, behind the publicity," she wrote, "I'm a girl trying to heal from something I am reminded of every day.

"It's a little easier now, but I'm not who I used to be. A part of my childhood was taken from me."

Minneapolis's to-do list is long. The COVID-19 pandemic again threw disparities into sharp relief: people of color, many with health conditions created by these gaps, were more likely to die. More than twenty-five hundred people died in the first two years of the pandemic in Hennepin County. It's the largest tally among counties, though a high vaccination rate also ranks it below the statewide level per capita. Still, COVID was seen as a major reason Hennepin County's population actually declined in 2021, for the first time in memory. Like the effects of George Floyd's murder, ramifications of the global pandemic will play out for years.

City of Minneapolis workers install signage for Bde Maka Ska Boulevard, October 28, 2019. *Minneapolis Park and Recreation Board*

The wealth gap keeps widening. Disparities persist in every measurement, from home ownership to birth outcomes. Younger people need opportunities; the middle class is disappearing; and the future of work, especially in downtown office buildings, is in limbo because of both the pandemic and the effects of automation.

Climate change is producing more intense storms, and temperatures in more northern latitudes generally are rising faster than elsewhere. Current trends suggest Minneapolis will have the shorter winter and warmer climate of present-day Kansas in sixty years. Studies have even found some cities, including Minneapolis, have measurably hotter temperatures in previously redlined areas. Blame less green space and more concrete in those neighborhoods.

These problems are not solely of Minneapolis's making, nor are they solely the city's to solve—they're deeply tied to national and global changes. But revisiting history is an important, early step in addressing disparities and inequities.

That's why, for example, a state law passed in 2019 gives homeowners a way to renounce racial covenants on their deeds. The covenants aren't enforceable, but their racist language still exists in thousands of records.

The city in 2019 also revamped zoning laws, which had been based on the original redlining maps. There was plenty of residential development in the first part of the twenty-first century, but very little of it required even a *portion* be affordable housing. Such housing remains scarce, leaving leaders facing the question of who actually gets to live in Minneapolis. The revamped laws aim to address gentrification by mandating that affordable housing units be included in new projects and by allowing denser development. Goals also include addressing eviction rates and renters' rights; city leaders are seeking ways to increase property ownership among African Americans, which was the lowest in the country among the eighty US cities with the largest Black populations.

As in other parts of the country, Minneapolis has addressed naming and memorializing controversies since 2018.

Lake Calhoun was restored to its Dakota name, Bde Maka Ska, in spite of a yearslong effort by opponents, one of whom asked (earnestly) in a newspaper commentary: "What exactly have the Dakota Indians done that is a positive contribution to all Minnesotans? What is the heroism or accomplishment that we are recognizing in order to justify renaming the lake to Bde Maka Ska?"

University of Minnesota regents initially rejected changing four buildings named for people whose actions, according to a task force, hadn't lived up to the ideals of an inclusive place. But a few years later, they adopted a process for renaming after seventy-five years, or earlier if warranted.

The Minnesota Twins removed a statue of longtime owner Cal Griffith in 2020 for the racist tirade he made (see chapter 10), and a street long named for eugenicist Charles Dight (chapter 7) was renamed in 2022 for John Cheatham. Cheatham was born enslaved in 1855 and became Minneapolis's first Black fire captain in 1899.

While these changes were not universally easy or quick to happen, they represented efforts to reflect more accurate and inclusive histories. Asking whether names bestowed by white settler-colonists should get a review is a way of reshaping what the city says about itself and who truly belongs in it.

Minneapolitans working to improve their city need to know *why* things are the way they are, and the results of that history are all around us. A postscript to the stories of Prince and the encampment at the Fourth Precinct police station after Jamar Clark's death in 2015 provides a great example.

It's hard to imagine Prince hadn't noticed the protests. The place was a familiar haunt. Before the police station, the community center called The Way had stood there. Born from racial tension decades earlier, the center offered many things, including a music program for neighborhood youth—like the teenage Prince Rogers Nelson.

The answers to today's crises require action—from all of us. But as you decide where to go from here, it's crucial to know how we got here. If you drive past a house in Linden Hills and remember it was once the scene of a race riot, you might better understand racial imbalances among the city's neighborhoods and schools. If you walk the Stone Arch Bridge and view St. Anthony Falls—Owamniyomni—while keeping their history in mind, you might better understand the area's spiritual sacredness to the Dakota and, later, its economic "sacredness" to white settler-colonists. Knowing the history of disparities in Minneapolis, you will always understand that Plymouth Avenue is not just any road on the north side and that 38th and Chicago isn't just another intersection.

Minneapolis's history includes collapses and constant rebuilding. The risks in rebuilding are inevitable: what if something fails again? But the biggest risk for the city lies in our making such decisions without first having built compelling, insightful connections to our sometimes forgotten past.

Author's Note

My great editor, Ann Regan, wanted a book that's both comprehensive and concise—literature's oxymoron. I've certainly left out more than I included here, but I believed in Ann's overall goal: to provide a brief overview of Minnesota's largest city for curious audiences.

I hope this book pushes you to learn more. Each chapter herein could be (and in many cases, is) its own book. I wrote this at a time when facts and logic seemed to matter less to more people. Making you want to learn more would be most satisfying.

There aren't as many comprehensive histories of Minneapolis as you might expect; it's been decades since the last. Projects like History-apolis (Augsburg University) and MNopedia (Minnesota Historical Society) have ably helped fill this gap. In my opinion, the Mapping Prejudice project at the University of Minnesota is the single most important recent gift to Minneapolis, offering previously ignored but crucial elements of the city's story. That project inspired me throughout this writing.

But there are limits. I am just the latest white man to tell the Minneapolis story, which skews—and continues the skewing of—such scholarship. Personal awareness only does so much, though it was important to me to start the story before Minneapolis existed. We are on Dakota land, and I suspect we newcomers don't get the best guest reviews.

I take seriously the responsibility of adding this book to the roster of histories. That subsequent histories might be built partially on what's written here seems more burden than honor, and I implore future historians to find their own paths in telling stories that remain untold.

For now, please allow some thank-yous, starting with the Hennepin County Library system for its resources and comfy places to work (shout-out to my home library, St. Louis Park). Elizabeth Hatle provided a crucial citation after COVID-19 shut libraries. Anne and Bryan lent office space. And many historians encouraged me.

Bill Green probably doesn't fully know how much I hang on his words for inspiration, nor does Kate Beane comprehend how much I've learned from her important work. Erika Lee offered advice at an especially important time, as did John Anfinson, a great Mississippi River historian. Thanks also to Jack El-Hai, Laura Weber, and Daniel Bergin for brief but appreciated encouragement. Andrea Swensson isn't just a great writer and historian; she's a dear friend whose cheerleading meant a great deal. Kirsten Delegard is doing important work with Mapping Prejudice and was gracious with advice—I hope readers of this book study her project next.

Thanks to Ann Regan, the Minnesota Historical Society, and its press, most of all for their patience. The Gale Library is a gem, and the Minnesota Department of Transportation has its own library—worth a visit!

This introvert discovered there's nothing more lonely, but also satisfying, than writing a book. I gained a wife during writing—in spite of, not because. Thank you, Peggy and Siobhan and my entire family for putting up with me these past months. I love you very much. The families of those listed herein also deserve thanks for their support. And thank you, readers, for supporting the work of a writer in your community.

For Further Reading

Most of the chapters in this book rely on these excellent books and articles, which provide both general background and in-depth treatment of specific periods: John O. Anfinson, *River of History: A Historic Resources Study of the Mississippi National River and Recreation Area* (St. Paul, MN: US Army Corps of Engineers, St. Paul District, 2003) and "Spiritual Power to Industrial Might: 12,000 Years at St. Anthony Falls," *Minnesota History* 58 (Spring-Summer 2004): 252–69; Peter DeCarlo, *Fort Snelling at Bdote: A Brief History* (St. Paul: MNHS Press, 2016); Lucile M. Kane, *The Falls of St. Anthony: The Waterfall that Built Minneapolis* (1966; repr., St. Paul: MNHS Press, 1987); Dave Kenney, *Twin Cities Album: A Visual History* (St. Paul: MNHS Press, 2005); Iric Nathanson, *Minneapolis in the Twentieth Century: The Growth of an American City* (St. Paul: MNHS Press, 2009); Shannon Pennefeather, ed., *Mill City: A Visual History of the Minneapolis Mill District* (St. Paul: MNHS Press, 2003); Andrea Swensson, *Got to Be Something Here: The Rise of the Minneapolis Sound* (Minneapolis: University of Minnesota Press, 2017); Gwen Westerman and Bruce White, *Mni Sota Makoce: The Land of the Dakota* (St. Paul: MNHS Press, 2012); Mary Lethert Wingerd, *North Country: The Making of Minnesota* (Minneapolis: University of Minnesota Press, 2010) and *Claiming the City: Politics, Faith, and the Power of Place in St. Paul* (Ithaca, NY: Cornell University Press, 2001). The graphics and articles at Mapping Prejudice (https://www.mappingprejudice.org) are an invaluable resource for Minneapolis history.

Readers interested in knowing more about Minneapolis history will find much of interest in the sources specific to each chapter that are listed below. These notes also provide sources for quotations.

Prologue

Quotations: Interview with Chris Mato Nunpa (p. 2, "Justice also has to happen"); *Star Tribune* (Minneapolis), October 28, 1987 (p. 2, "the year the Twins").

1. Bdote

Walt Bachman, *Northern Slave, Black Dakota: The Life and Times of Joseph Godfrey* (Bloomington, MN: Pond Dakota Press, 2013); William Green, *A Peculiar Imbalance: The Fall and Rise of Racial Equality in Minnesota, 1837–1869* (St. Paul: MNHS Press, 2009); Zebulon Pike, *The Expeditions of Zebulon Montgomery Pike* (New York: Dover, 1997).

Quotations: Steven Return Riggs, *Dakota Grammar, Texts, and Ethnography* (Washington, DC: US GPO, 1893), 164 (p. 7, "The Mdewakanton think"); Ella Deloria, *Speaking of Indians* (1944), 24–25 (p. 8, "The ultimate aim"); Louis Hennepin, *A New Discovery of a Vast Country in America* (1699; repr., New York: Kraus, 1972), 54 (p. 10, "this horrible precipice"); Anfinson, "Spiritual Power," 253 (p. 10, "first act"); W. E. Hollon, "Zebulon Montgomery Pike's Mississippi Voyage, 1805–1806," *Wisconsin Magazine of History* 32 (1949): 447 (p. 13, "naive, egotistical"); 34 Cong., 1st sess., serial 836, US Senate Military Affairs Committee Report 193, 3 (p. 14, "there is no evidence"); John C. Calhoun, *The Works of John C. Calhoun* 5 (New York: D. Appleton, 1851–57), 38 (p. 14, "When these posts"); Westerman and White, *Makoce*, 182 (p. 17, "ceased to be"; full quote is at *Ratified treaty no. 258, documents relating to the negotiation of the treaty of July 23, 1851, with the Sisseton and Wahpeton Sioux Indians* [July 23, 1851], 41); Nathaniel West, *The Ancestry, Life, and Times of Hon. Henry Hastings Sibley* (St. Paul, MN: Pioneer Press Pub. Co., 1889), 263 (p. 18, "eat grass or their own dung"); *Red Wing Extra Session, Message of Governor Ramsey to the Legislature of Minnesota, Delivered September 9,*

1862 (St. Paul, MN: Wm. R. Marshall, 1862), 12 (p. 18–19, "The Sioux Indians"); DeCarlo, *Fort Snelling*, 61 (p. 21, "As the white man").

2. St. Anthony Falls

William D. Green, "Eliza Winston and the Politics of Freedom in Minnesota, 1854–60," *Minnesota History* 57 (Fall 2000): 106–22.

Quotations: Kane, *Falls of St. Anthony*, 7, 32–33 (p. 25, "I should not be surpris'd," and p. 31, "our only neighbors"); R. L. Cartwright, "Eliza Winston Court Case," MNopedia.org (p. 26, "restrained of her liberty").

3. Timber, Then Flour

Kevin Ehrman-Solberg, "'Minneapolis Is Ruined': The Tunnel Disaster of 1869" and "The Minneapolis Riverfront: An Underground History," Historyapolis.com; Molly Huber, "St. Anthony Falls Tunnel Collapse, October 5, 1869," MNopedia.org. Coverage of the I-35W bridge collapse, including stories published in later years, appears in articles at *Minn-Post, Star Tribune*, Minnesota Public Radio, and ESPN.

Quotations: Frederic Trautmann, "Johan Georg Kohl: A German Traveler in Minnesota Territory," *Minnesota History* 49 (Winter 1984): 133 (p. 36, "The water being"); Anfinson, "12,000 Years," 259 (p. 38, "mere whitlings").

4. Immigration and Corporate Growth

Karen Cooper, "Minstrelsy in Minnesota," *MinnPost*, February 8, 2019; Kirsten Delegard, "Bohemian Flats," Historyapolis.com; Don L. Hofsommer, *Minneapolis and the Age of Railways* (Minneapolis: University of Minnesota Press, 2005); Charles M. Loring, "History of the Parks and Public Grounds of Minneapolis," *Collections of the Minnesota Historical Society* 15 (1915): 599–608; Kate Roberts and Barbara Caron, "Advertising in the Mill City, 1880–1930," *Minnesota History* 58 (Spring-Summer 2003): 308–19; Marion Daniel Shutter, ed., *History of Minneapolis: Gateway to the Northwest* 2 (Chicago, Minneapolis: S. J. Clarke, 1923); Donald Woods, "Playhouse for Pioneers: The Story of the Pence

Opera House," *Minnesota History* 33 (Winter 1952): 169–78. On racial covenants, see www.mappingprejudice.org.

From MNopedia.org: R. L. Cartwright, "Artificial Limb Industry in Minneapolis"; Aaron Hansen, "St. Paul and Pacific Railroad" and "Great Northern Railway"; Molly Huber, "Stone Arch Bridge, Minneapolis" and "De la Barre, William (1849–1936)"; Janet Meyer, "Minnesota Orchestra"; and David C. Smith, "Loring, Charles Morgridge (1833–1922)" and "Cleveland, Horace William Shaler (1814–1900)."

Quotations: Bruce M. White, "The Power of Whiteness, or, The Life and Times of Joseph Rolette Jr.," *Minnesota History* 56 (Winter 1998–99): 190 (p. 50, "of a mixture"); Writers' Program of the Work Projects Administration, *The Bohemian Flats* (1941; repr., St. Paul: MNHS Press, 1986), 48 (p. 59, "What can a man do").

5. Rivals!

Jack El-Hai, "The Census War," *American Heritage* 41 (July-August 1990): 106–9; Molly Huber, "Industrial Exposition Building, Minneapolis," MNopedia.org; Charles A. Lindquist, "The Origin and Development of the United States Commissioner System," *American Journal of Legal History* 14 (January 1970): 1–16; C. A. Nimocks, *The Early History of the Minneapolis Parks, from 1857 to 1883* ([Minneapolis]: N.p., 1911); Mark Twain, *Life on the Mississippi* (1883).

Quotations: Wingerd, *Claiming the City*, 14 (p. 63, "the two cities"); John T. Flanagan, "A French Humorist Visits Minnesota," *Minnesota History* 40 (Spring 1966): 15 (p. 63, "are near enough").

6. The Corrupt Doc and a Lost Reputation

Edward H. Bennett, Andrew Wright Crawford, and Civic Commission of Minneapolis, *Plan of Minneapolis* (Minneapolis: Civic Commission, 1917); Curt Brown, "Minnesota History: The Great Minneapolis Fire of 1893," *Star Tribune* (Minneapolis), April 2, 2015; Kirsten Delegard, "A Cancer at the Heart of the City," Historyapolis.com; William Millikan, *A Union Against Unions: The Minneapolis Citizens Alliance and Its Fight Against Organized Labor, 1903–1947* (St. Paul: MNHS Press, 2001); Vincent

Oredson, "Planning a City: Minneapolis, 1909–17," *Minnesota History* 33 (Winter 1953): 331–39; Marjorie Pearson, "Approaching the Capitol: The Story of the Minnesota State Capitol Mall," *Minnesota History* 65 (Winter 2016–17): 120–35; Erik Rivenes, *Dirty Doc Ames and the Scandal That Shook Minneapolis* (St. Paul: MNHS Press, 2018); Lincoln Steffens, "The Shame of Minneapolis," *McClure's* 20 (January 1903): 227–39; Colin Woodard, *American Nations: A History of the Eleven Rival Regional Cultures of North America* (New York: Viking, 2011). For articles at MNopedia.org, see Linda A. Cameron, "Twin Cities Streetcar Strike, 1917," and Tamantha Perlman, "Ames, Albert Alonzo "Doc" (1842–1911)."

Quotation: Wingerd, *North Country,* 240, 241 (p. 71, "New England of the West").

7. Discrimination, Redlining, and the KKK

"Acknowledging Racial, Discriminatory Historical Practices on UMN Campus," *Minnesota Daily,* February 17, 2019; Tim Brady, *Gopher Gold: Legendary Figures, Brilliant Blunders, and Amazing Feats at the University of Minnesota* (St. Paul: MNHS Press, 2007); David Mark Chalmers, *Hooded Americanism: The History of the Ku Klux Klan,* 3rd ed. (Durham, NC: Duke University Press, 1987); Kirsten Delegard, "Tracing the City's Anti-Semitic Past," March 13, 2015, *The Journal,* journalmpls.com; Elizabeth Dorsey Hatle, *The Ku Klux Klan in Minnesota* (Charleston, SC: History Press, 2013); Ann Juergens, "Lena Olive Smith: A Minnesota Civil Rights Pioneer," *William Mitchell Law Review* 28 (2001): 397–453; Greta Kaul, "With Covenants, Racism Was Written into Minneapolis Housing," *MinnPost,* February 22, 2019; articles at MappingPrejudice.org; Eric Roper, "Why Were So Many of Park Avenue's Original Mansions Torn Down?" *Star Tribune* (Minneapolis), June 14, 2019; Charles Rumford Walker, *American City: A Rank and File History of Minneapolis* (1937; repr., Minneapolis: University of Minnesota Press, 2012).

From *Minnesota History*: Sarah Atwood, "'This List Not Complete': Minnesota's Jewish Resistance to the Silver Legion of America, 1936–1940," 66 (Winter 2018–19): 142–55; Elizabeth Dorsey Hatle and Nancy M. Vaillancourt, "One Flag, One School, One Language: Minnesota's

Ku Klux Klan in the 1920s," 61 (Winter 2009–10): 360–71; Gary Phelps, "The Eugenics Crusade of Charles Fremont Dight," 49 (Fall 1984): 99–108.

From MNopedia.org: Linda A. Cameron, "Agricultural Depression, 1920–1934"; Peter J. DeCarlo, "Smith, Lena Olive (1885–1966)"; Mark Haidet, "Minneapolis Flour-Milling Industry during World War I"; Heidi Heller, "Phyllis Wheatley House, Minneapolis"; Dave Kenney, "Origins of the NAACP in Minnesota, 1912–1920"; Denise K. Lajimodiere, "Native American Boarding Schools"; Paul Nelson, "Blumenfeld, Isadore 'Kid Cann' (1900–1981)"; Matt Reicher, "Minnesota Commission of Public Safety."

Quotations: John Rosengren, "A Football Martyr," November 25, 2014, SBNation.com (p. 80, "My thoughts"); Kirsten Delegard, "Race War Continued: Linden Hills, 1909," Historyapolis.com (p. 81, "black people should avoid" and "the residents of Linden Hills"; p. 84, "know they are undesirable"); "Race War Started in Prospect Park," *Minneapolis Tribune*, October 22, 1909 (p. 82, "We are not here to argue"); Laura Weber, "'Gentiles Preferred': Minneapolis Jews and Employment, 1920–1950," *Minnesota History* 52 (Spring 1991): 182 (p. 88, "hard fact"); Office of the Historian, Foreign Service Institute, US Department of State, "The Immigration Act of 1924," https://history.state.gov/milestones/1921-1936 (p. 88, "preserve the ideal"); Nathanson, *Minneapolis*, 98 (p. 90, "the most successful use"); University of Minnesota, "Report of the Task Force on Building Names and Institutional History," February 2019, https://university-history.dl.umn.edu/ (p. 90–91, "The races have never").

8. Battles

Dick Bancroft and Laura Waterman Wittstock, *We Are Still Here: A Photographic History of the American Indian Movement* (St. Paul: MNHS Press, 2013); Thomas Blantz, "Father Haas and the Minneapolis Truckers' Strike of 1934," *Minnesota History* 42 (Spring 1970): 5–15; Alexia Fernandez Campbell, "How America's Past Shapes Native Americans' Present," *The Atlantic*, October 12, 2016.

From MNopedia.org: Ehsan Alam, "Minneapolis Teamsters' Strike, 1934"; Tom O'Connell, "Humphrey, Hubert H. (1911–1978)"; Kara Sorensen, "Twin Cities Army Ammunition Plant"; Margaret Vaughan and Harlen LaFontaine, "Indian Reorganization Act in Minnesota"; Laura Weber, "Mount Sinai Hospital and Foundation, Minneapolis"; Anja Witek, "Dunne, Vincent Raymond (1889–1970)."

Quotations: David Paul Nord, "Minneapolis and the Pragmatic Socialism of Thomas Van Lear," *Minnesota History* 45 (Spring 1976): 10 (p. 98, "shattered any idea"); Walker, *American City*, 165 (p. 99, "We are going to"); Charles Lindbergh, "Des Moines Speech," September 11, 1941, http://www.charleslindbergh.com/americanfirst/speech.asp (p. 102, "the three most important groups"); James Lileks, "Minnesota Moment; 'Smith of Minnesota' Was an Early Gopher State Football Miracle," *Star Tribune* (Minneapolis), February 1, 2018 (p. 104, "If six million"); Dave Kenney, *Minnesota Goes to War: The Home Front during World War II* (St. Paul: MNHS Press, 2009), 19 (p. 107, "We Indians fought"); Gary Reichard, "Mayor Hubert H. Humphrey," *Minnesota History* 56 (Summer 1998): 52, 58 (p. 110, "Are you hoarding," and "one of the four or five"); Nathanson, *Minneapolis*, 107 (p. 112, "most comprehensive"); Kirsten Delegard, "Racial Housing Covenants in the Twin Cities," MNopedia.org (p. 115, "By the time"); Minnesota, Governor's Interracial Commission, "The Indian in Minnesota: A Report to Governor Luther W. Youngdahl of Minnesota," April 1, 1947, [4] (p. 116, "Within Minnesota"); Ben Nighthorse Campbell, "Activating Indians into National Politics," in George Horse Capture, Duane Champagne, and Chandler C. Jackson, eds., *American Indian Nations: Yesterday, Today, and Tomorrow* (Lanham, MD: AltaMira Press, 2007), 2, 3 (p. 117, "if you can't"); Travis M. Andrews, "In Rare Interview, Bob Dylan Holds Forth," *Washington Post*, March 23, 2017 (p. 120, "I thought the only").

9. Urban Not-So-Renewal

Kirsten Delegard, "A 'Disturbance Born of Disillusionment': 50 Years of Black Lives Matter on Plymouth Avenue," Historyapolis.com; Larry Millett, *Twin Cities Then and Now* (St. Paul: MNHS Press, 1996); Richard

Rothstein, *The Color of Law: A Forgotten History of How Our Government Segregated America* (New York: Liveright, 2017); Swensson, *Got to Be Something Here* and "It Was 50 Years Ago Today That the Beatles Played in Minnesota," August 21, 2015, blog.thecurrent.org.

From MNopedia.org: Britt Aamodt, "Foshay Tower," "HIV/AIDS Crisis, 1981–1997," and "Positively Gay Cuban Refugee Task Force"; Ehsan Alam, "Rondo Neighborhood, St. Paul"; Lizzie Ehrenhalt, "Minnesota Amendment 1"; Jon Lurie, "American Indian Movement (AIM)"; Susan Marks, "Civil Unrest on Plymouth Avenue, Minneapolis, 1967"; Jack Matheson, "Spear, Allan Henry (1937–2008)"; Iric Nathanson, "Minneapolis Skyways"; Paul Nelson, "Dayton's"; Kate Roberts, "Southdale Center"; Sarah Shirey, "*Baker v. Nelson*"; Brianna Wilson, "AIM Patrol, Minneapolis."

Quotations: Kenney, *Twin Cities Album*, 211 (p. 123, "I hated it"); Larry Millett, *Metropolitan Dreams: The Scandalous Rise and Stunning Fall of a Minneapolis Masterpiece* (Minneapolis: University of Minnesota Press, 2018), 6 (p. 123, "The future generations").

10. Voices Heard

Kirsten Delegard, "A 'Disturbance Born of Disillusionment,'" Historyapolis.com; Bruce Johansen, "Out of Silence: FREE, Minnesota's First Gay Rights Organization," *Minnesota History* 66 (Spring 2019): 186–201; Gail Langer Karwoski, Michael McConnell, and Jack Baker, *The Wedding Heard 'Round the World: America's First Gay Marriage* (Minneapolis: University of Minnesota Press, 2016); "Same-Sex Marriage Celebration Brings Hundreds to Minneapolis City Hall," *Minnesota Daily*, August 7, 2013; "Listen to Minnesota Musicians Perform Prince Hits Outside First Avenue," thecurrent.org, April 25, 2016.

From MNopedia.org: Joy K. Lintelman, "Swedish Immigration to Minnesota"; Sharon Park, "Immigrants and Refugees in Minnesota: Connecting Past and Present" and "Indochinese Refugee Resettlement Office, 1975–1986"; Anduin Wilhide, "Somali and Somali American Experiences in Minnesota."

Quotations: Swensson, *Got to Be Something Here,* 5, 7, 180, 186 (p. 135, "up and down Hennepin"; p. 137, "On the surface"; and p. 150, "it was a very" and "Even though 'Funkytown'"); Nick Coleman, "Griffith Spares Few Targets," *Star Tribune* (Minneapolis), October 1, 1978 (p. 136, "I'll tell you why"); Iric Nathanson, "Martin Luther King's '63 and '67 Minnesota Visits," January 16, 2012 (p. 139, "had rectified some evils"), and "Remembering Charlie Stenvig and the Minnesota T Party," June 16, 2010 (p. 140, "take the handcuffs off")—both at MinnPost.com; Clyde Bellecourt with Jon Lurie, *The Thunder Before the Storm: The Autobiography of Clyde Bellecourt* (St. Paul: MNHS Press, 2016) (p. 140, "men in our community"); Joshua Preston, "Senator Allan Spear and the Minnesota Human Rights Act," *Minnesota History* 65 (Fall 2016): 76–87 (p. 145, "Let me tell you"); Maureen O'Boyle, interview with John L. Nelson (Prince's father), *A Current Affair,* 1991, https://www.youtube.com/watch?v=Byr-TaMiogA (p. 149, "because I wanted him"); Dan Piepenbring, "The Book of Prince," *New Yorker,* September 9, 2019 (p. 149, "I went to school" and "In retrospect"; and p. 152, "I stayed in Minneapolis").

11. Refugee, Rebirth, and Reconciliation

Jon Jeter, "Murderous Toll in an Unlikely City," *Washington Post,* November 25, 1995; Trista Raezer-Stursa, "Coyle, Brian J. (1944–1991)," MNopedia.org; Kimmy Tanaka and Jonathan Moore, "Fuji-Ya, Second to None," *Minnesota History* 66 (Fall 2018): 98–111.

Quotations: Personal interview with Mukhtar Ibrahim (p. 153, "joyous moment"); Ben Jacobs, "Somali Migrants Are 'Disaster' for Minnesota, Says Donald Trump," *The Guardian,* November 7, 2016 (p. 153, "disaster taking place"); Miriam Elder, "Donald Trump Got Really Personal at His First Rally of the Impeachment Era," October 11, 2019, BuzzFeedNews.com (p. 154, "a disgrace to our country"); Faiza Mahamud and Jessie Van Berkel, "Somali-Minnesotans Wonder About Their Welcome After Trump's Speech," *Star Tribune* (Minneapolis), October 11, 2019 (p. 154, "I didn't know we were hated"); Mitch Smith and Christina Capecchi, "'This Creates Fear': Trump Rally Turns Spotlight on Minnesota's Somali Community," *New York Times,* October 15, 2019

(p. 154, "I think it's someone"); Anne Panning, "Anne Panning Reflects on Minneapolis, Minnesota," *Newsweek,* October 29, 2012 (p. 156, "Haight-Ashbury"); Iric Nathanson, "Riverside Plaza: One More Effort to Revive a 'New Town—in Town,'" August 4, 2010 (p. 158, "New Town in Town"), and "How a 1972 Report Laid the Groundwork for Minneapolis' Riverfront Revival," July 5, 2017 (p. 159, "the backside")—both at MinnPost.com; R. T. Rybak, *Pothole Confidential: My Life as Mayor of Minneapolis* (Minneapolis: University of Minnesota Press, 2017), 207 (p. 163, "Much of north Minneapolis").

12. Saying Their Names

Quotations: Jonathan Allen, "It Wasn't Right," Reuters, March 30, 2021 (p. 165, "It wasn't right"); Exhibit207072020.pdf, filed in District Court State of Minnesota, July 7, 2020 (a transcript of the police call) (p. 166, "Mom, I love you,"); "Prosecutor Ends Rebuttal Argument in Chauvin Trial," *The Hill,* April 19, 2021 (p. 170, "You are told"); Zoe Strozewski, "Charges Won't Be Filed," *Newsweek,* April 6, 2022 (p. 171, "this tragedy"); "Minneapolis Mayor Frey Admits to Being Misleading," WCCO, February 7, 2022 (p. 171, "more casual"); Minnesota Department of Human Rights, "Investigation into the City of Minneapolis and the Minneapolis Police Department," April 27, 2022, mn.gov/mdhr (p. 171, "City and MPD leaders"); Justin Ellis, "Minneapolis Had This Coming," *The Atlantic,* June 9, 2020 (p. 172, "When you're born").

Epilogue: What Next?

Jeremiah Bey Ellison, "'Woe Is You,' White People Keep Telling Us," *New York Times,* April 15, 2020.

Quotations: "Darnella Frazier, Who Filmed George Floyd's Murder, . . ." NPR, June 11, 2021 (p. 173, "highlighting the crucial role"); Michael Miller, "Counterpoint: What Did the Dakota Contribute to Minnesota?," *Star Tribune* (Minneapolis), November 2, 2017 (p. 175, "What exactly have").

Index

Italicized page numbers indicate a photo or illustration or its caption.